All in All

JAMIN ANNE HART

WOODSONG
PUBLISHING

All In All

Jamin Anne Hart

Copyright © 2025

Most Scripture quotations are from the King James Version of the Bible unless otherwise identified.

Some Scripture quotations are marked NIV and are taken from the New International Version of the Bible. New International Version®, NIV®. Copyright © 1973, 1978, 1984, 2011 by Biblica, Inc.™ Used by permission of Zondervan. All rights reserved worldwide.

Some Scripture quotations are marked ESV and are taken from the the ESV® Bible (The Holy Bible, English Standard Version®), copyright © 2001 by Crossway, a publishing ministry of Good News Publishers. Used by permission. All rights reserved.

Some Scripture quotations are marked ESV and are taken from the New King James Version®. Copyright © 1982 by Thomas Nelson. Used by permission. All rights reserved.

All rights reserved. This publication may not be reproduced, stored in an electronic system, or transmitted in ny form or by any means, electronic, mechanical, photocopy, recording, or otherwise, without proper credit to the author. Brief quotations may be used without permission.

ISBN 978-1-961482-17-3

Cover Design by Jeremy Hart for Hart Creative + Design

Published by Woodsong Publishing (Seymour, IN)

Printed in United States of America.

Dedicated to

my son, Graham Hudson Hart.

You have brought us a deeper purpose, love,

and joy we knew not existed.

contents

chapter one
Saved By The Alarm...9

chapter two
So, This Is Love... 25

chapter three
Choosing That Good Part 39

chapter four
Hey, Wanna Bake With Me?.. 53

chapter five
Superheroes Source Of Strength.. 65

chapter six
Idle Days In Patagonia.. 79

chapter seven
If You Had a Say, Where Would This Road Lead?................ 97

chapter eight
Hidden In The House 111

chapter nine
The Journey Is Worth It All 127

CHAPTER ONE

saved by the alarm

My son was nine days old the night Jesus spared our lives. Did you know that? I have a son now! It began as a somewhat ordinary day. Although recovering from a c-section had not been on the birth agenda, somehow the cuddles from my newborn made it as pleasant as it could be. My mom and sister had made the trek from Minnesota to Oklahoma to help cook, clean, and give lots of love to the newest family member. As I sat in my living room chair with baby in arms, I smiled as the aromas of freshly baked chocolate biscotti and a home-cooked dinner filled our home. Yet the greatest scent of all was the intoxicating newborn smell from the baby I cherished so closely within my arms. God had indeed been good to us.

I was also overwhelmed with gratitude for family who show up in support through every season of our lives. We now live next door to my in-laws, and we invited them over to partake of a relaxing evening with all of us together since my mother had made a feast for dinner. About five minutes before Jeremy's parents arrived, our carbon monoxide detector started making itself known, loud and clear. We were in disbelief when the dispatcher from our security system came on our security hub asking if she could send the fire department. We told her we had been cooking all day, the house

Saved By The Alarm

had gotten hot, and everything seemed to be okay. Not seconds after our dispatcher had cleared the alarm on our security hub hanging on our kitchen wall, our other carbon monoxide detector began to beep incessantly and persistently on the other end of the house. What a scene for my in-laws to walk into! As Jeremy and my father-in-law investigated the obnoxious beeping more closely, trying to identify if the four rapid beeps meant carbon monoxide, a wave of heat and tiredness washed over me. I liken it to a wave, yet it didn't pass, and it was much more persistent than a "newborn tired;" it felt like I could soon pass out. My mother-in-law looked at me and asked, "Jamin, are you okay?" Still holding my baby, I got up and began to walk for fear I was going to fall asleep or much worse, lose consciousness. As my mom continued to get the food out of the oven, this strange feeling would not leave me, and we soon realized this may not be a false alarm. We called the fire department with a new urgency and fled from our house to Jeremy's parent's house next door. What a sight we were! Wrapping my son tightly in warm blankets, I walked as fast as a woman recovering from a c-section dared to walk. I held Graham while the rest filled their hands with dishes of the four-course meal we planned to eat next door. Our breath froze in the air; we didn't know to laugh hysterically or cry from panic.

I still couldn't shake the feeling, that foreboding feeling of weakness and unconquerable lethargy. I fought it fervently. I asked the looming question, "But if there was carbon monoxide in our house, we made it out in time, right?" My voice shook only slightly. "I sure hope so," was the matter-of-fact voice of my sweet mother-in-law.

Now a new level of panic hit me. My son! My family! Jeremy and his dad were still over at our house with the fire department, and we ladies had huddled on my in-law's deck to get fresh air in our lungs. Shivering more from fear than cold, we waited until the first responders appeared. Still fighting the overwhelming sleepiness, the fireman told me the news we all dared not believe: "Ma'am, we did find carbon monoxide in your house. The highest levels were found in your bedroom." The bedroom was located right next to the chair I had been sitting in all day! He began to take my vitals as I shivered out words in utter panic, "I… want… Jeremy!" If I was going to die, I sure wanted my husband with me! My mother-in-law raced off to retrieve him.

Soon, Jeremy appeared on the deck, hugging me for a minute, assuring me in his calm way everything would be okay. Then he stepped back and grabbed the rail of the deck for support. As the fireman began to ask him a question, Jeremy paused with a glazed look and said, "Now I'm feeling it, too."

"Sir, you need to sit down!" the fireman shouted. He saw what we all saw, my husband was a second away from passing out. He stumbled to the closest deck chair and laid his head back. Now the fireman was taking my husband's vitals. With pure adrenaline, I felt no pain as I jumped out of my chair to be at my husband's side. Voices told me to sit down as I was recovering from a major surgery, but I didn't care. I was worried about my strong husband who was about to pass out. Before we could register what was happening, the fire squad had called for two ambulances, and more firemen and paramedics appeared. As I was being helped onto the ambulance stretcher, one ambulance worker yelled, "Give the mom the baby!"

Saved By The Alarm

Jeremy was being loaded onto another stretcher. "Can I ride with my husband?" I managed to croak out in between shivers.

"No, ma'am, that's not how this works," came the reply. Well, it wasn't like I was up to date on ambulance protocol—I had never ridden in one, for goodness sakes! It was as if I had a front row seat to a dramatic play, for surely this was not happening in my own life.

They allowed my mom to ride with me, and my sister rode with Jeremy. My vitals were very high, which is no surprise with such panic. I was strong for my baby son, who was fast asleep through it all as I held him with shaky arms in the ambulance. My mom sat close by, offering strength and comfort as well. The woman in the ambulance talked with us to help calm the situation and handed me a very large stuffed animal. "This is for your son. We give these to all the kids who ride in here, but he is the youngest we have ever had." I didn't know what to say to that. They mentioned his oxygen was low, and my heart began beating faster.

When we arrived at the ER, we were quickly rolled through the ambulance entrance, and the EMT by my side kept promising me I could see my husband as quickly as possible. Although the ER was busy, by the favor of God, we were all able to be put together in a room. Nurses bustled about, and soon all three of us were getting our blood drawn to be sent immediately to the lab for testing. The foreboding question, "What if the levels are too high in our body?" was suddenly overcome by something greater—our prayers. Although nurses were still busying themselves in and out, I cared not. One cares less about appearance when life itself is on the line. As I held an oxygen mask to my nine-day old's tiny face, I began to pray out loud. Not a quiet patty-cake prayer, either. I began to plead the blood of Jesus over my husband, over my son, and myself. I claimed every promise, I declared this was not the end! A holy boldness came over us, and we spoke the name of Jesus, we prayed with passion, and what could have been a room of heaviness soon became a room of God's peace. My husband and I began to encourage each other in the Lord. What the enemy meant for evil, to try to take us and our new son, we knew God was about to turn for good! In fact, this just convinced me that God has something extremely special for our son's life and ours, as well! This was not the end.

With new hope rising higher than the carbon monoxide levels, the doctor finally came in with the ultimate news: "The carbon monoxide levels are at 3.7 and 3.8 in your bodies. Your body can't handle anything above a five, and since it is below that, you all are going to be all right." He continued, "I'm glad this is the news I am giving you; it could have been a lot worse. I just had to give another family very different news. You got out just in time." The highest levels detected in our house were in the bedroom. If we had gone to sleep as planned after dinner, we never would have woken up. We were saved by the alarm. We were kept by the protecting power of God.

We were released well after midnight, and when our house was inspected and cleared of all poisonous gasses, we finally fell asleep in the early hours of morning, knowing God has us safely in His hand. We placed the stuffed animal Graham had been given in his nursery. One day we will hand him this stuffy and tell him how God saved his life when he was nine days old. Oh, the thoughts He has toward us, thoughts of peace and not of evil, to give us a future and a hope. The next day we found His sweet peace and laughter in our home where there could have easily been trauma. What a gift to be in the hand of the Lord, covered by His blood!

THE STRENGTH OF HIS COVERING

Amid a generation screaming at us and our children, "Be strong! You alone are all you need!" it is no wonder the masses crumble under the pressure and find themselves at strange places of confusion. We were never created to be strong enough on our own, we were created to be in covenant relationship with our Creator. He is not the author of confusion, rather of clarity and strength to everyone who seeks His face. We need Him! Do you think my husband and I felt strong with the looming news of carbon monoxide poisoning? Of course not! But that's the comfort of living in obedience to His Word. We leaned upon His never-ending strength while waiting anxiously within that sterile emergency room. We spoke His promises, we thanked Him for salvation, we praised Him for being our Master!

APPLYING THE BLOOD, CONSUMING THE LAMB

I didn't need such a drastic moment to remind me—although remind me it did—I need Jesus. I need His peace, His protection, His covering. It is not a debatable part of life; it is life itself. My family and I must be covered by the blood of Jesus and protected by His Name.

There has always been a means of covering for God's people. In the Old Testament, before Calvary and the message at Pentecost, God sent a man named Moses to be a sounding alarm to deliver a saving message. Even still today, He often uses a man of God to sound the alarm in our lives. It was a choice of obedience available equally to all:

> *"Your lamb shall be without blemish, a male of the first year. And they shall take some of the blood and put it on the two doorposts and on the lintel of the houses where they eat it. Then they shall eat the flesh on that night; roasted in fire, with unleavened bread and with bitter herbs they shall eat it. Do not eat it raw, nor boiled at all with water, but roasted in fire. You shall let none of it remain until morning, and what remains of it until morning you shall burn with fire. And thus you shall eat it: with a belt on your waist, your sandals on your feet, and your staff in your hand. So you shall eat it in haste. It is the Lord's Passover… Now the blood shall be a sign for you on the houses where you are. And when I see the blood, I will pass over you; and the plague shall not be on you to destroy you when I strike the land of Egypt."*
> Exodus 12:5-13 ESV

For Israel to be spared the judgement of the firstborn, they had to apply the blood just as God instructed.

> *"Then Moses called for all the elders of Israel and said to them, "Pick out and take lambs for yourselves according to your families, and kill the Passover lamb. And you shall take a bunch of hyssop, dip it in the blood that is in the basin, and strike the lintel and the two doorposts with the blood that is in the basin. And none of you shall go out of the door of his house until morning. For the Lord will*

Saved By The Alarm

> *pass through to strike the Egyptians; and when He sees the blood on the two doorposts, the Lord will pass over the door and not allow the destroyer to come into your houses to strike you."*
> Exodus 12:21-23 ESV

Applying the blood would take careful consciousness. These men did not grab any old lamb found limping around and prepare the sacrifice any carefree way. There are no loopholes, shortcuts, or quick fixes; God's way is accurate and undeniably specific. To do His commands shows a devotion and commitment specifically toward Him. It leaves no question or confusion of who one serves and will always be opposite of the world's way. Yes, it takes work and separation to apply the blood and consume the Lamb, nor can it be done half-hearted. There is no escaping personal investment and attention to detail but thank God for it. This careful obedience is what saves us!

For the Israelites, I daresay there were no grumbles murmured in the home regarding the sacrifices of animals. Surely there was a mother who cried out with relief, "I'm so glad we have been given instruction on what to do. What mercy! Whatever sacrifice it takes, it's worth it. My firstborn will live and not die!" There was undoubtedly a father who uttered not one complaint as he went about the business of finding and preparing a spotless lamb. As young siblings clung at their mother's skirts, I can see no fear on their faces, only smiles at the glorious thought, "We are all going to live! My mommy and daddy are obeying the saving instructions for our home. We will live and not die!"

ALL IN ALL

NEW TESTAMENT APPLICATION

If our homes are to be covered by God's favor, we must still consume the Lamb and apply His blood to our lives. Because of Calvary, the resurrection, and the instruction on the day of Pentecost, we know now it is not physical blood from a Lamb we paint on our doorposts. For indeed Christ, our Passover Lamb, was sacrificed for us *(1 Corinthians 5:7)*. John the Baptist drew on a similar image when he said of Jesus, *"Behold! The Lamb of God who takes away the sin of the world!" (John 1:29)*. In The New Testament, we are given a saving alarm through the Apostle Peter. We must apply Christ's blood in baptism and be consumed with the Lamb, being filled with His Holy Spirit inside of us!

> *"Then Peter said unto them, Repent, and be baptized every one of you in the name of Jesus Christ for the remission of sins, and ye shall receive the gift of the Holy Ghost."*
> Acts 2:38

When we live in obedience to Him, we find great peace knowing whatever comes our way—and whatever the outcome may be—our life is in the hands of Almighty God! We give God praise, for we know it was He alone who spared our home and firstborn son that blustery December night; the night we were saved by the alarm.

SAVED BY THE FIRE ALARM

Little Cloe was only five years old when she saved her blind grandmother. Shortly before, she had taken a field trip to the local fire station, learning specifically what to do in the event a fire alarm

Saved By The Alarm

sounded. Soon after, she had her chance to put the knowledge to use. One evening while she was staying with her grandmother, the stove caught on fire. But thankfully for little Cloe, when the alarm sounded, she knew exactly what to do. With inward knowledge for such a time as this, she quickly got her grandmother out of the house, then proceeded to run to the neighbor's house to call 911. Lives were saved that night because a five-year-old girl knew the importance of responding in obedience to the fire alarm. Their loud, persistent sounds are not something to be loathed, rather it is a life-giving gift! Even children know the truth, alarms are created to save our lives.

Our Heavenly Father has given us the greatest sounding alarm of all to save us from our own eternal fire. He has given us the Word of God and free will to obey Him. Every directive is still true, His plan of salvation is still necessary, and the victory is still sure—but only if we listen to the sound.

THANK GOD FOR THE ALARM

What if five-year-old Cloe would have refused to adhere to the alarm? What if we would have shut out the noise of our carbon monoxide alarm? The ending is almost too sobering to think about. Thank God for the alarm! We cannot afford to ignore that certain sound of God's Word sent to warn us about this world's devastating ending. It rings a warning against the culture's hot topics of the day, swiftly leading us back on the narrow path lest we fall prey to believing such heresy.

The world will say God's alarm is demanding, difficult, distracting, and outdated. They declare it comes on at the most inconvenient times, calling for action no flesh wants to make. Yet I thank God for the inconvenient moments of interruption, for within them are clear words that save us from destruction, distraction, disillusion, and disappointment. 2 Timothy 3:16 says, *"All Scripture is given by inspiration of God, and is profitable for doctrine, for reproof, for correction, for instruction in righteousness," (NKJV)*.

Truth will always sound like hate to those who despise it. So when culture proclaims, "Who needs a pastor? There are no absolutes—no truth—just be your own truth," we recognize it as a blaring alarm, warning us to seek what truly saves.

> *"For whosoever shall call upon the name of the Lord shall be saved. How then shall they call on him in whom they have not believed? and how shall they believe in him of whom they have not heard? and how shall they hear without a preacher?"*
> *Romans 10:13-14*
>
> *"I am the way, the truth and the life."*
> *John 14:6*

Time does not change the validity of His truth. "Jesus Christ the same yesterday, and to day, and for ever," *(Hebrews 13:8)*. Thank God for the alarm!

When the world props up ungodly leaders and stars, professing them as "good," we must hear the resounding alarm, lest we ourselves believe such a thing!

Saved By The Alarm

"Woe unto them that call evil good, and good evil; that put darkness for light, and light for darkness."
Isaiah 5:20

"There is none good but one, that is, God."
Mark 10:18

We must remember that He is our very definition and standard of everything good; therefore, if it doesn't align with Him, by definition it cannot be called good. Thank God for the alarm!

When agendas cry, "You can decide what gender you are!" the Word reverberates as a signal to save us from confusion:

"So God created man in His own image; in the image of God He created him; male and female He created them."
Genesis 1:27

When TV shows, books, and media portray fun as children who sneak around, lie, and disobey parents, Scripture resonates with the sounds of an alarm!

"Thou knowest the commandments... do not bear false witness... Honour thy father and mother."
Mark 10:19

When the crowds taunt, "You're the only one not joining us! Come on, try it, and be a part of us," we hear the clanging of the lifesaving alarm,

> *"Wherefore Come out from among them, and be ye separate, saith the Lord, And touch not the unclean thing; And I will receive you, And will be a Father unto you, And ye shall be my sons and daughters, saith the Lord Almighty."*
> 2 Corinthians 6:17-18

Oh, how His Word protects His children! Thank God for the alarm!

There is no hopelessness found in Him. Through obedience comes the privilege of not only a divine relationship with a loving Savior, but protection from the One who holds all power. When we apply His Word to our life, it becomes a shield to spare us from the fiery arrows of painful confusion and ungodly worldviews. Family units stay strong in obedience. Children rise up and call mothers blessed. Husbands praise their wives. Workers are raised up before kings. When our ways please the Lord, even our enemies are at peace with us. When we lie down, we will not be afraid; our sleep will be sweet.

Our songs are joyful, our comfort is sure. There is divine blessing in obedience! And to think, it is all because God loves us enough to give us an unexpired alarm for all time. We are still saved by the Word of God!

CHAPTER TWO

so, this is love

I heard my son's voice for the first time the afternoon of November 28, 2023. My birth story ended in an abrupt and unplanned c-section, and I shall never forget hearing the tiny cry from behind the surgical curtain and my husband saying in my ear, "Hear that, babydoll? That's our son!" A moment later, the nurse brought him around, and I beheld the tiny miracle I had carried within me the past nine months.

I was stunned when I saw the perfection of him. His reddish curly hair, his arresting blue eyes, those pruny looking fingers, his intoxicating smell, and that attractive little mouth. Overcome by an unexplainable emotion and distracted from all discomfort, I could only repeat softly to my husband and little baby, "He's so cute! He's so perfect! Oh, you are so perfect."

I can testify to the truth of what they say: it is worth it all the moment you see your baby. I felt I was almost in a trance as I beheld him, for this hardly could be my reality. We were smitten with an unconditional love the moment my husband and I laid eyes on our son. How I felt I knew him so well yet had never officially met him before—a paradox to say the least but with his earth-side arrival something of wonder awakened in me! I now held the very hands and feet that had kicked inside of me for months on end. I now

Saved By The Alarm

kissed the little mouth that had slipped out hundreds of tiny hiccups within my womb. I was a mother, and I knew in this moment that no matter what success I might hold in life, "wife" and "mother" were the highest titles I could ever claim.

I couldn't wait to spend a lifetime getting to know his personality, likes and dislikes, strengths and weaknesses. For whatever they may or may not be, we knew our love for him would not change. This tiny newborn had done no action to earn our love, yet we would die for him simply because he was ours. We now had a son! And our world suddenly felt complete.

A NEW DISCOVERY

It took only about ten days for us to realize Graham either had extreme colic or something else was upsetting him more than the usual newborn discomforts. His cries would not only last for hours in the evenings but soon continued throughout the duration of the day. As we wracked our brains about what could be causing such great discomfort, we switched to dairy-free formula in hopes that might produce relief. When that provided no evident change, we continued to try several other formulas, all holding their own hope to solve the situation. We found ourselves continuously trying every tip and trick out there to calm a newborn's upset stomach. When all proved to no avail, the next few weeks only brought more cries which became continuous, almost constant, and full of discomfort.

We found little to no sleep due to his days and nights still mixed up. On top of the lack of sleep was the misery of hearing our child cry out for hours without reprieve. We experienced feelings of helplessness that shook us deeply. What an awful feeling of inadequacy to hold no solution for our own flesh and blood. Although both sets of our parents were supporting us in any way they possibly could, this new season felt lonely, leaving us utterly drained and exhausted.

With each passing day, I found myself falling more in love with my husband and held an even deeper appreciation as I watched his character—steady and consistent—go above and beyond to help care for our family. He not only was present with Graham, he was also taking care of me as I recovered from a major surgery and at times couldn't even get out of bed without a helping hand. I knew we shared the exhaustion and pain equally for we are a team, and I couldn't imagine carrying this load with anyone else.

Since Graham had his days and nights mixed up for so long, my husband offered to get up with him every other night, which allowed us both to get uninterrupted sleep for a few hours. On my nights I would often crumble into tears, unable to bear Graham's constant cries alone. I would tense up, only escalating the situation, but how could I bear to see his small body hurting? I would wake my husband, and he would come to my side, willing to bounce Graham in his arms, as we prayed again. Many evenings we anointed his head with oil, believing for an answer, a miracle, a reprieve from the tears that shattered us all. We prayed he would fall into a peaceful sleep and when he awoke, this would all be behind us.

However, there were some nights within those eight weeks I did manage to stay awake, letting my husband sleep, slowly pacing our halls with our baby. Constant movement and bouncing were our best tools to comfort his cries and seemed to help as much as anything else. I was left feeling robbed of any joy from the newborn

So, This Is Love

stage. I fought strong feelings of jealousy: jealous of the mothers who held their newborns on outings without apparent stress, those who had recovered well, those who slept well and rarely heard their baby's painful cry. My poor baby had never been able to sleep through one church service or even a quick coffee stop without crying in discomfort, leaving me to retreat to a private room, hurting and confused. Yes, my mind fought many thoughts but to put it simply, I just felt robbed and depleted.

A SONG IN THE MIDNIGHT HOUR

What do we do when the answer hasn't arrived and we find no other choice but to walk through the dismal season? Our steps will lead us somewhere, so they might as well lead us to the King of Kings. How we have prepared in our yesterday is what we are able to produce in our today. How thankful I am that we had cultivated a lifestyle of worship in our yesterday; therefore, it was only second nature to run to a place of praise in our present storm. Since I was in a fight with many thwarting thoughts, I decided to fight the only way I knew would produce victory: I began to worship and praise the Lord. I would turn on a song of praise in my living room, and night after night, without the strength to hardly sing the lyrics for myself, I spoke the lyrics:

> "And the angels cry holy, all creation cries, holy. You will always be, holy, holy forever." (Holy Forever by Chris Tomlin)

Although outwardly my situation would not change for a few more weeks, the atmosphere would shift when from a broken heart

I declared Him to be what He always will be: Holy forever, my all in all. Somehow, when we move our focus to Glory itself, we find that in Him we can make it one more day. He is equally worthy of a song of praise in the midnight's darkness just as He is in the glory of morning's light.

THE IMPORTANCE OF A SONG

Allow me a moment to remind us of this truth: it matters what songs we allow our ears to hear. Music was created in heaven, designed for worship to God alone. Satan, as he does with all things, has twisted music's original design to try to bring glory to himself instead. Songs have the power to become deeply and inescapably ingrained in someone's memory, a phenomenon referred to as an "earworm". There is a reason teachers have put the ABCs and other important information in song form: it is a known and proven fact our minds are able to bring to remembrance song lyrics quicker than mere spoken words.

We are only able to produce what we have planted, so how can we sing a song of praise and deliverance if it is not rooted within us? How we prepare in our yesterday is how we will perform today; therefore, if we have only filled our heart and mind with songs and lyrics that do not lift up the name of Jesus or encourage our spirit, our songs in the night are powerless to bring deliverance. What we allow ourselves to sing will either bind us with chains or break our chains.

Paul and Silas sang praises unto God in a prison cell at midnight, and the fetters couldn't help but fall when God was glorified! Miriam and Moses sang a song of deliverance, Hannah

So, This Is Love

sang a song of thankfulness and praise, and David sang songs of rejoicing, so how can we suggest what we sing has no real impact on us? To debate with the doubters desiring to ease their own conscience is not my purpose. I share only my personal testimony of victory and what the Word of the Lord says on such a topic:

> *"Speaking to yourselves in psalms and hymns and spiritual songs, singing and making melody in your heart to the Lord."*
> Ephesians 5:19

So, in my midnight, I sing a song that declares Him to be what He has always been: my healer, my deliverer, my God, my strength, my help, my holy and wonderful King. He's all I needed when I didn't have a baby, and He's all I need with our baby. He was my all when I walked through a season of glory, and He's all I need when I can only see the fire. When Jesus is with us, we can look back with a testimony, "Although I walked through the fire, I can't even smell the smoke upon me now!"

A WORD IN THE MIDNIGHT HOUR

Undoubtedly there were times during the two months before the answer arrived that felt almost unbearable as we privately cried right along with our son. We had reached out to multiple people, and no one seemed to be able to figure out what was going on. In some ways, I had never felt this low before, nor had my heart carried such concern.

My husband and I were exhausted physically, mentally, and emotionally—although we held tightly to each other, we didn't see how we could bear it for much longer. Helplessness drains a body like nothing else, and we felt we were well on our way to our wit's end. Yet weary and worn out as we were, we knew we would not stop until we found the answer for him.

One particular night as I held my newborn son in my arms, I pulled up the picture on my phone the nurse had snapped for us. It captured the first moment of his birth on the other side of the surgical curtain. It is one of my favorite pictures; he was red-faced yet adorable, screaming away. I knew his six-week-old mind wouldn't comprehend what I was saying, but I showed him the picture, and in the wee hours of the morning, I spoke these words: "Graham, you were crying the moment I first saw you and fell in love with you. It meant you were alive! I want you to know your tears or the amount thereof do not change my love for you. Mommy and daddy will love you, no matter what." When I finished my quiet speech to my son, it was me that had tears running down my face, for I felt the Lord gently speak to my heart, *"And that is just how I feel about My children."* It was a reminder, a reminder I desperately needed, of the unconditional love of our Creator. When we find ourselves weary from caring for others, we still have an all-powerful God who is caring for us. When we are holding our children, our Heavenly Father is holding us.

I must admit in this season there had been times I felt purposeless and desperately weak. I am normally a pretty high-energy person who loves ministry, movement, fun, and pouring into others. Yet I had no strength for any of that now; it was a season where I shed more tears than I care to recall, needing assistance simply to make it to another day. When I feel I am not bringing much to the table, or when I am sick, I can feel downright less lovable. But that is not how our Heavenly Father sees us, and His reminder came quickly as an anchor in my midnight, just when I wondered if the waves or worry might overtake me.

Perhaps you also have found yourself in a season where your emotions and problems feel an annoyance, even to your closest loved ones. Weakness surely has a way of making us feel embarrassed. Yet let me remind you, dear reader, we have a Heavenly Father who is drawn toward our weakness. It is there when His presence and Word become our anchor, a bond is forged that cannot be easily severed. How He longs to show forth His might to His children!

> *"For the eyes of the LORD run to and fro throughout the whole earth, to show Himself strong on behalf of those whose heart is loyal to Him...."*
> 2 Chronicles 16:9 NKJV

We detest storms, yet where else can we hear His powerful voice speak to the very crashing elements around us, "Peace, be still," and all things become still? There is an appreciation and thankfulness for the One who walks with us through the fire and through the storm. No wonder David said these words in Psalm 119:

> *"It was good for me to be afflicted so that I might learn your decrees. The law from your mouth is more precious to me than thousands of pieces of silver and gold. Your hands made me and formed me."*
> Psalm 119:71-73 NIV

Thousands of pieces of silver and gold can do nothing for us in such a moment, but His powerful presence changes everything. It is there we are reminded His hands have formed us; therefore, we know He alone has the power to renew our mind and joy!

When I have found myself grappling with a traumatic experience, through Him I have been able to overcome it. He was there with me through the fire, and now I can look back even on the scariest moments of my life and declare, "I don't even smell the smoke on me!" Only the One who has created us can perform such a miracle within us!

Depression, discouragement, disaster, and disease do not dictate His love toward us. He is not a man that He should lie, rather in Him there is no shadow of turning. He gently stays by our side, proving in the fire and storm to be Wonderful, Counsellor, the mighty God, the everlasting Father, the Prince of Peace. He provides exactly what we need in every circumstance of life—whether it's a friend, strength, open doors, a church, or opportunities. He is everything! The amount of our tears will never change His love toward His children. Thanks be to God!

THE ANSWER

It was not until Graham was over eight weeks old—eight weeks that stretched on for eternity—when the answer was finally found by a doctor. He was not only allergic to dairy but soy as well, and one or the other was found in everything we had been giving him. No wonder his small stomach was in painful fits, he was unable to process what we had been feeding him. How my heart broke for him to have suffered when the answer proved so simple, yet I felt

So, This Is Love

a wave of relief for the discovery! Although we cannot pretend to understand God's timing, the Lord led us to the right doctor who took the time to find the answer. We now hold tightly to another reminder of His faithfulness in our own life.

SHELTERED IN THE ARMS OF GOD

From April to December of Graham's first year of life, we took him on forty-nine flights. Talk about an evangelist baby! I was reminded of a truth in every new place. I found whether we were in a chaotic airport, mall, doctor's office, crowded restaurant, or the blustery outdoors, it mattered not to our son. When we held him in our arms, he didn't bat an eye of concern about our location. He fiercely trusted his parents to protect him while he slept in peace. Location or circumstances mattered little; his only focus was the connection and comfort he found from the presence of his parents. He found great safety sheltered in our arms.

We, too have the same glorious privilege as the children of the Most High God. It matters not our location, only our connection with our Heavenly Father.

> *"Whoever dwells in the shelter of the Most High*
> *will rest in the shadow of the Almighty.*
> *I will say of the Lord, 'He is my refuge and my fortress,*
> *my God, in whom I trust.' Surely he will save you*
> *from the fowler's snare and from the deadly pestilence.*
> *He will cover you with his feathers, and under his wings you will*
> *find refuge; his faithfulness will be your shield and rampart.*

You will not fear the terror of night,
nor the arrow that flies by day."
Psalm 91:1-5 NIV

THE MIRACLE OF A CRY

Accompanying the many lessons and surprises that came when I became a mother was the innate instincts and intuitiveness to my son's voice and needs. I quickly found I could be in a deep sleep, yet when my newborn babe made even the softest cry, I would immediately awaken and spring to his side to attend to his needs. It mattered not if it was the fifth time he woke before five o'clock, when I heard his husky little cry come forth for milk or comfort, you better believe I was next to him in spite of blurred vision and puffy eyelids.

How I love him!

I now understand in a new light how God's ear is in tune to my cry, and that He is by my side to meet my needs, even in the midnight hours. I am not a burden to my Heavenly Father.

The miracle of a newborn cry means breath is in their lungs, and it is a reason to rejoice. In whatever stage of life we may find ourselves, there is still a miracle found within, for we can take comfort in this: When we cry out to God, we will receive an answer. As long as I have breath in my lungs, I will worship Him. His ear is turned to His children's cries, and that is a miracle I will never take for granted.

"The righteous cry out, and the LORD hears them; he delivers them from all their troubles."
Psalm 34:17 NIV

So, This Is Love

"Behold, the LORD's hand is not shortened, That it cannot save; Nor His ear heavy, That it cannot hear."
Isaiah 59:1 NKJV

"The eyes of the LORD are on the righteous, And His ears are open to their cry."
Psalm 34:15 NKJV

If even the bird's cry brings forth the immediate attention of our Lord, how much more does our Father come to comfort, hold, and strengthen you and me?

SO, THIS IS LOVE

Today, I find the challenging newborn season only a memory in the rear-view mirror. He has miraculously outgrown every allergy, and now I am gazing ahead as I chase my energetic, charming, and healthy toddler as he explores the bright world around him. Our little family is vivaciously loving life more than ever!

How thankful I am for the love and support of our family and closest friends, a good doctor, and my husband who never wavered. Yet above all I rejoice in my God. Now, I can look back and see how he carried our heaviness every step of the way.

He proved once again His ear is always open to the cry of His children. He does not sleep nor grow weary and always is willing to come to save us. Indeed, throughout the first year of my son's life I have learned in a new and profoundly deep way what love really looks like. Profound, yet simple: Love is simply God in our midst!

CHAPTER THREE

choosing that good part

I didn't like myself. Have you ever felt that way? I didn't like my attitude, how I felt, how I looked, nor how I was treating my family. The worst part of it was it happened to be my first Mother's Day's weekend, and to put it simply, I was being snippy with my loved ones and miserably exhausted.

As an evangelist wife, every year we find ourselves somewhere new, and this particular Mother's Day we were preaching in Boise, Idaho. In place of excitement, the long travel days and culminating sleepiness was drowning me. Graham had entered his worst sleep regression yet, waking six times a night, and I couldn't help but ponder the question, "How do people expect moms with infants to function in life, anyways? We weren't made to only get three or four hours of sleep a night!" It all felt a bit unfair to me, and although I could try to justify it through my sleepy stupor, the reality was I was fixating on all the wrong things.

It culminated Mother's Day morning. Even with waking up to flowers, coffee, and my favorite perfume on the hotel's nightstand, thoughtful gifts could not undo what was about to implode. I didn't care about anything except the desperation for sleep and a break from bottles and diaper changes. I must admit in my morning scramble to pack the diaper bag, get Graham and

Choosing That Good Part

myself ready for church and out the door, I hadn't had time to pray, much less open my Bible. Come to think of it, I hadn't the last couple days, either.

We didn't have time to snap a Mother's Day picture before church, and no sooner than service begun, Graham had a rare but extremely evident blowout. Good thing I had packed some extra pajamas in his diaper bag! After the clean up, I attempted to be present back in the service, but soon my baby let his voice be known it was well past his nap time. There was no nursery, so I retreated to the pastor's office, dealing with disappointment from feeling removed from hearing my husband's Mother's Day sermon he had worked so hard on. There I sat in the rocker that was placed in the paster's office, trying to get my little one to sleep. I felt isolated. As I stared into Graham's precious face, I did manage to have some prayer time, but soon I began dozing off in the quiet. Oh, how I longed for a break to get some sleep! I did my best to focus, soak in, and appreciate the moment for what it was. I tried to remind myself there are some who would give anything, including the lack of sleep, to live my life. Yet exhaustion has a way of robbing even the best of times.

After church, social media did what it does best, and the comparison game was almost too much for my disillusioned, sleepy state. Graham was now in some mix-matched pajamas, and I was feeling far from the glowing mothers on my screen. Surely their babies were angels during all of service, I noted with remorse—as if social media has ever shown the full story!

The mom guilt was growing at rapid speeds and when nap time didn't happen back at the hotel, all emotions came pouring out at once. If we were to label what took place next, a "glorified meltdown" is to put it mildly; I felt I had nothing else to give and my heart ached. My kindhearted husband, who I knew was exhausted himself, ended up taking the whole night shift so I was able to get a full night's rest.

Even still, as we packed up the next morning, my attitude was only worse. Patches of silence and mini-meltdowns left me once again neglecting my time with the Lord. After all, I was busy caring for Graham's needs and trying to pack up another hotel room. I dreaded the flight to Washington we planned to board later that afternoon; I was exhausted to a level I never imagined one could feel. I was miserable, and the attitude I was choosing to live in was even worse than the tiredness I felt.

THE PRAYER

Although we were pushed on time, my husband encouraged me to stop everything and spend time with Jesus. We couldn't keep functioning like this; my discouragement was affecting everyone around me. I went to the bedroom and knelt. I felt a bit angry and once I finally spoke, it was a raw prayer. "Lord, I don't even like myself right now. I'm miserable. I feel like I'm getting nothing done, and I can't even sit through a whole church service these days. I hardly feel like myself and let me add, evangelizing with a baby is much harder than I thought it would be! Is it too much to ask for some peace and sleep?!"

Hormones and feelings were valid, but I was fighting against my reality, and when that happens, disaster and misery are always present. The more I thought about my problems, the

Choosing That Good Part

more depressed I got. Yet when I spoke aloud my frustrations in His presence, a glorious sense of release and peace settled within. I felt His nearness, and in His gentleness toward me I couldn't help but surrender even the deepest part of my heart. When I did, something beautiful happened: My prayer shifted. "Lord, just as you touched Isaiah's mouth with the coal, come and do it for me. Cleanse my heart. I am desperate and want your renewing, refreshing, and cleansing. My husband and baby do not deserve this. You are so good, Lord, and I need you." I felt His presence cover me, and I spoke aloud for quite some time in a heavenly language. Feeling encouraged, I wiped my eyes and felt the Lord impress a thought into my heart. *"When you serve your son, you are serving me."* I quickly remembered the scripture:

"And whatever you do, do it heartily, as to the Lord and not to men." Colossians 3:23 NKJV

I felt lighter as I clung to His word and laid down my burdens at His feet. The Lord saw everything I was doing, and it wasn't "nothing" to Him; it was everything I needed to be doing in this season. Although I didn't catch up on sleep instantaneously, I found a rest my soul had been crying out to receive.

After such a holy moment, did it make my situation suddenly easy? No, when I rose from my knees, I was still in the thick of sleep regression woes and surviving full-time travel with a tiny one. But I can tell you this: It carried me through! The Lord heard the cry of my heart and without judgement or condemnation, He showed Himself true to His Word:

"He will feed His flock like a shepherd; He will gather the lambs with His arm, And carry them in His bosom, And gently lead those who are with young."
Isaiah 40:11 NKJV

THE CHOICE

There is always a spiritual and practical application. I felt reminded that although I undoubtedly received a spiritual renewing, it was up to me to rise from my knees and continue to choose to dwell upon the positive. God did what only He can do, and as I sincerely asked Him, "How can I change how I feel today?" I felt the answer in my heart, "Dwell upon my Word." That is something only I can choose to do.

We must never forget the truth written in Psalms:

"Blessed is the man... his delight is in the law of the Lord, and in His law he meditates day and night. He shall be like a tree planted by the rivers of water, That brings forth its fruit in its season, Whose leaf also shall not wither; And whatever he does shall prosper."
Psalm 1:1-3 NKJV

What we choose to dwell upon has instant impact for our daily outcome. We often rise from our knees facing circumstances we cannot control, yet we always have control over our mindset. I rose from my feet, choosing to dwell on His Words, choosing to dwell near Him.

Choosing That Good Part

DAVID CHOOSING JOY IN DISCOURAGEMENT

In Psalm 13, We find our beloved King David discouraged and depressed.

> *"How long shall I take counsel in my soul, Having sorrow in my heart daily? How long shall mine enemy be exalted over me?"*
> Psalm 13:2

No wonder David was discouraged! Taking counsel in his own soul had led him to daily sorrow in his heart. How often our humanity tries to take control of the situation! Our outcome only becomes more depressing and disastrous until we choose to rejoice in the presence of God. David came face to face with such a choice: He could continue to dwell in his sorrow—exalting his enemies, fear, and worries—or rejoice at the feet of God. But David chose to rejoice!

> *"My heart shall rejoice in thy salvation. I will sing unto the Lord."*
> Psalm 13:5-6

David directed his feelings instead of allowing his feelings direct him. He told his heart to get busy rejoicing! When David felt he had no other reason to be joyful, he rejoiced in the salvation of God. This is solid ground for any believer. When we are saved, we can command our heart to start rejoicing in Him!

CHOOSING JOY

You know what? When I, too, chose to dwell upon the Word of my Lord and the joy of His salvation, even in my sleepiness, my joy overflowed. Oh, the change that covered our little family when my mindset aligned with His Word and I made up my mind to choose a heart of rejoicing!

What could have been another day of a rotten attitude and grouchiness shifted into a day of peace. I now reminisce about the day with great fondness! Once we left the hotel, we had breakfast with the pastor, and when Graham got fussy, I stayed calm and chose to embrace the moment. Although my food got cold, I walked about the restaurant rocking him in my arms, and soon he calmed down.

I can recall with a smile how we stopped by a bookstore where I picked out a book to read to him. We then found a gourmet cookie shop, and after Jeremy purchased a double chocolate cookie for me, I sat in the backseat with Graham, reading him the new Curious George book as my husband drove us to the airport. As we hummed along the highway in our rental car, listening to worship music, we all felt a peace that passed all understanding. In place of earlier misery, I now couldn't stop thinking of the goodness of God in my life. Taking time to be at the feet of Jesus changed my whole day.

People may wonder from the outside why we give our life to Jesus, but it is no chore to me. It is something unexplainable till experienced; truly, one must taste and see for themselves! I want to live my life as a testimony so others may see there is peace available throughout every season within a joyous relationship with our Heavenly Father. To me, this inward peace is one of the greatest gifts He gives His children. A heavenly gift He allows us to hold on this earth, and it can only be given by God and nothing compares to it.

Choosing That Good Part

> *"Peace I leave with you, My peace I give to you; not as the world gives do I give to you. Let not your heart be troubled, neither let it be afraid."*
> John 14:27 NKJV

Throughout the remainder of that day, I kept my mind upon God's word and felt His comfort and nearness. Even when in my flesh I didn't "feel" like it, how thankful I was for choosing time at the feet of my Jesus!

MOTHERS IN THE BIBLE

That day in Idaho, I couldn't help but think of Mary, the very Mother of Jesus. Did she escape the pains of delivery and the newborn stage altogether just because she was chosen and loved by God? No, but I believe she clung to the Word of the Lord, and it carried her through! What about faithful and pure-hearted Hannah? Did she somehow dance around discouragement within her barrenness and harassment from Peninnah because she loved the Lord? No, but she knew how to kneel in prayer, and when she arose, she had a word from God that carried her and brought unspeakable joy on the other side. Did Hagar, who was unfairly rejected, escape living in the wilderness season all together? Not at all, unfortunately; however, she received a word from God and it carried and fed her along with her son to a place of growth and peace, even in a wilderness.

CHOOSING THAT GOOD PART

There is a time recorded in Luke 10 where Martha graciously opened her home to a large gathering of people. Jesus was there along with the disciples and other guests, and just like any good host, Martha wanted everything to be perfect. As happy as she was to open her home, in all of her bustling about she began feeling overwhelmed with the amount of work to be done. Surely, we can understand that! Many guests meant much food to be cooked, dishes to be hand washed, and people to entertain. In the busyness of tasks, she became more consumed with the cumbersome load of serving than the Savior dwelling in her home. In Martha's mind, she felt she had no choice but to serve alone with much worry. Soon her frustration turned to the younger sister, Mary, who, instead of helping her, was sitting at the feet of Jesus.

She let it be for a while, but soon Martha could not handle it anymore. She approached Jesus, but it was frustration and not adoration that came bubbling over. Luke 10:40 says, *"But Martha was cumbered about much serving, and came to him, and said, Lord, dost thou not care that my sister hath left me to serve alone? bid her therefore that she help me."*

Jesus spoke His gentle response unto Martha: words of correction indeed, but out of an abundance of love and understanding. Verse 41 says, *"Martha, Martha. Thou art careful and troubled about many things."*

I am sure she mentally agreed immediately. Of course, she was careful and troubled about many things! Aren't we all? She felt the weight personally of hosting such an event; How could she not be troubled and careful? She was trying to be a blessing and only found herself overwhelmed and drained instead. Life does have a way of bringing us more work than what we originally signed up for!

But as He finished his sentence in verse 42, we see Jesus gently

Choosing That Good Part

reminding her and all of us, *"but one thing is needful: and Mary hath chosen that good part, which shall not be taken away from her."*

Though His words were a correction, they were in no way indicative of one personality type being better than the other, or of one sister being favored above the other. His words were only a simple yet shaking reminder that work without worship should never happen.

It is of course natural for us to be responsible and dedicated to our household duties, career, commitments, even ministry. That is a necessary part of life! Yet Jesus was setting the record straight: In all of life's troubles, in all of our being careful, planning, and making of schedules, there is one thing that is most needed. Make sure we daily choose to spend time at Jesus' feet. We must be in fellowship with our Creator!

Why, you might ask, must we choose that good part? Because how quickly our daily choices turn into habits, and soon our habits shape who we are at our core, our very character affecting every part of our well-being. What we receive at His feet is inward, not an object we hold in our hand to be taken out by force or coercion. No one can steal what we receive in His presence unless we willingly hand it over. Every good and perfect gift comes from above and there is no one good but God, so it only makes sense every good part in our lives must come from Him! He longs to pour upon us new mercies daily: Good gifts from above, and a renewed mindset. I must be in His presence to receive it!

There, He gives us a peace where we know all things will work together for our good, an inward joy that is not dictated by circumstances, and a love that is not dependent on those around us.

ALL IN ALL

What we receive in His presence is that good part where no devil in hell, no agenda in this world, no force of darkness, or bitter enemy can take from us. When we choose to carry His light within us, even our present darkness cannot snuff it out unless we choose to allow the darkness to blow within us.

THEY CHOSE THE GOOD PART

When the demon possessed man in the graveyard at Gadara, as imperfect and possessed as he was, chose that good part and fell and worshiped at the feet of Jesus, no thousands of devils could take away the deliverance and calling he received.

When Peter, although consumed with a past of mistakes, chose that good part, no lying voice of guilt and condemnation could take the forgiveness and purpose he received when He fell at the feet of Jesus and worshiped Him.

As for the woman with the issue of blood, miserable from fighting pain and embarrassment of her grotesque and perhaps visible disease, no one could deny the healing she received when she chose that good part, made her way through a crowd, and fought her way to the feet of Jesus. *"If I may but touch the hem of his garment, I will be made whole!"*

For the wise men, no exhaustion of a journey could keep them from choosing that good part. They continued to follow the light, and the moment they saw their Savior in the manger, they fell down at His feet in worship to Him. No daunting journey could take the joy they received of simply being in His presence. It is in His presence where we still find fullness of joy, and at His right hand are still pleasures forevermore.

Choosing That Good Part

Solomon, the wisest earthly king, was no exception from choosing that good part. When the temple was completed, in front of the gathered congregation of people, he chose that good part. The Bible says in 2 Chronicles 6 verse 13, *"he kneeled down on his knees and worshiped."* When he finished praying, the Bible tells us fire came down, and the glory of the Lord filled the temple. No onlooker or doubter can take away our experience of Holy Ghost fire and the blessing of being in the midst of the glory of the Lord. There is no fulfillment we can find in this world that compares to choosing that good part that cannot be taken away from us!

"Oh come, let us worship and bow down, let us kneel before the Lord our maker."
Psalm 95:6

We may face what we deem unfair circumstances at times, but we are never exempt from experiencing His goodness in every part of our lives. This joy that I have, the world cannot give it, and the world cannot take it away. Even within the busyness of motherhood, I choose the good part that cannot be taken from me!

CHAPTER FOUR

*hey,
wanna bake
with me?*

I should have known I was pregnant the moment I burst into tears when my brother-in-law, Andrew, told me I was bad at mini-golf. Although "emotion" could be my middle name, this seemed a bit extreme, even for me. There I was visiting family in Raleigh, North Carolina, and I could not seem to keep the tears from dripping down my face on the mini-golf course; I was indeed having a meltdown over miniature golf. Once my husband told me as kindly as possible "you need to get it together," I stumbled through the remainder of the game with the best attitude I could muster. Thank goodness an ice cream shop was next on our agenda. I must have eaten my feelings because four scoops later I was feeling almost back to myself.

Two weeks later we found out the jovial news: I was pregnant! Although my pregnancy somehow dodged morning sickness altogether, what it didn't dodge was pregnancy cravings. I used to think those were only a silly excuse to get whatever one desired in pregnancy until I found myself cooking a full-blown spaghetti dinner from scratch at three-thirty in the morning.

This particular night I had laid wide eyed in bed with only one thing on my mind: homemade spaghetti and garlic toast. Not just any old recipe, the kind my mom used to make with spicy Italian

Hey, Wanna Bake With Me?

sausage. Out of complete luck—or God's humor—we happened to have every single ingredient needed for such a dish. So, knowing I wouldn't get a wink of sleep until this dream came to fruition, I crept into the kitchen, as my husband lay fast asleep, to create a culinary masterpiece. I tried to keep the banging of pot and pans to a minimum as I threw tomato sauce, oregano, fresh garlic, and parmesan into one bubbling creation, with the meat and noodles cooking away in the other pans. What a sight I must have been when at four in the morning I sat by myself at the kitchen table, enjoying helpings of a high carb meal in utter silence. This was not my usual diet, which made it all the more humorous! As I finished the large portion with a happy sigh, I moused back to bed and fell fast asleep, feeling as if I didn't have a care in the world.

A few weeks later, another craving struck. My husband and I hit the hay this particular night at midnight. This was pretty usual for us due to the late nights we were used to with our evangelizing schedule. It happened innocently enough: My husband saw a picture on his phone of a donut and made the passing, casual comment, "That donut looks good." Something rose up in me. "Let me see!" Glancing at the dense and carb-filled rotund dessert, I informed my husband, "Jeremy, I want that donut. Now." He laughed and moved on with the conversation, but I circled back around. "Oh my goodness, I need a chocolate frosted donut with rainbow sprinkles!"

His logical voice broke through my dreams. "Jamin, it's midnight. There's no way you can get one."

Because our phones always seem to be listening to provide a targeted ad, sure enough, an ad on social media popped up on his phone, this time the donut being complete with chocolate icing and sprinkles. Jeremy laughed. I began to cry. "I need that donut! Specifically, a cheap gas station one!"

He looked at me, stunned. "Are you serious?"

"Yes!!" I looked pitiful, I know.

"Well, I guess you can call the gas station down the street."

So, now well past midnight, I dialed the number with adolescent eagerness, and in the most childlike voice I asked the lady in the other end, "Do you have chocolate donuts with sprinkles?" There was a pause—surely she was trying to figure out if this was a prank call—then answered as nicely as she could, "No ma'am, we are sold out this late..."

"Thank you," I managed to speak before hanging up and bursting into tears. At this point I was laughing with my husband through my tears because I knew how ridiculous this was, but oh how I also knew my life might depend on getting one of those donuts!

Being the loving husband he is, Jeremy finally said, "I guess you could call the QT gas station that is further away, and if they have donuts, I'll drive and get them for you."

It took me less than a minute to find the number to call and ask the same faithful question, but this time, to my pregnancy delight, the answer came back, "Yes ma'am we just stocked our donut case full."

Could this be true? It must be for the late-night truckers—or expectant mothers! True to his word, my husband jumped in the car and drove to the gas station at one in the morning to get me not one large and fattening donut, but three of them. He brought back the chocolate one with sprinkles, along with an apple fritter and a

Hey, Wanna Bake With Me?

maple glazed. I destroyed two and a half out of the three, and after a joyful hug to my husband, I snuggled up and fell immediately into a peaceful sleep. When I woke up the next day, I suppose part of me regretted wasting hundreds upon hundreds of calories on cheap gas station donuts, although it is a story we will always remember. Our son is now here, pregnancy is in the rearview mirror, and I have not had spaghetti or gas station donuts since that day. What strange and hilarious times we find in our pregnancy adventures!

Whether we are pregnant or not, let's be real: Sometimes we just need a little treat. Although I try to maintain an active and healthy lifestyle even while being on the road full-time, I still have to have my chocolate close by. When I need to recharge, I often escape to my kitchen, turn on a podcast, worship music, or a beloved Adventure in Odyssey, and get to baking one of my most decadent desserts. Now that is therapeutic!

CHILDHOOD MEMORIES

Surely, we can all recall a time where we found ourselves in someone's home while they were baking fresh bread or pastries. Perhaps it is what draws us to bakeries; it immediately brings to us warm and wonderful feelings of comfort.

It should be no surprise some of my fondest memories within my childhood years was knowing my mom was puttering in the kitchen, creating a pan of tasty treats for her family. Greater than the aromas and promised sweet treats that I knew awaited me was the peaceful, relaxed atmosphere that seemed to always accompany it. I will cherish the lighthearted days where I played with my miniature Winnie the Pooh toys in the living room while my mom was bustling about in the kitchen. Often, she would be listening to worship music or an audio drama while she worked, the stories always uplifting and interesting.

Among her specialties were her chocolate chip cookies. I vividly remember one night later in my teenage years when I found myself overwhelmed with adolescent "boy problems" and unable to fall asleep. I crept downstairs to the kitchen where I knew my mom had just made a fresh stash of cookies. Sitting in our living room I opened my Bible and ate several of those glorious chocolate chip cookies. Something about a homemade dessert from a loved one, accompanied by hope and encouragement, has a way of healing many things. I also remember a time at college, seven hundred miles from home, when I received a package from my mom in the mail. It was a batch of those homemade chocolate chip cookies and a sweet note. I will never forget how loved she made me feel with that simple yet priceless package, somehow making my momentary problems vanish.

Truly, baking for friends and family has become one of my love languages. To share such goods has a way of bringing equal delight and comfort to the receiving soul and to the giver!

THE BREAD OF LIFE

The reality is a loaf of bread will eventually be consumed with only crumbs as evidence, and baked goods and their aromas have expiration dates. Yet these were the words of Jesus:

> *"I am the bread of life. Whoever comes to me will never go hungry, and whoever believes in me will never be thirsty."*
> John 6:35 NIV

Hey, Wanna Bake With Me?

Throughout the Scriptures, baking represents God's provision for His people. From the manna (bread) in the wilderness poured down from heaven upon His people, to the bread shared among five thousand men plus the women and children, God continually provided the needs of His people. Their recipe for bread, full of nutrition and often containing sweet figs and spread with raw honey, was quite different than the store-bought loaves and sugary jams of our day. It was the fullness of a meal, so when Jesus said He is the bread of life, it became clear to all those listening that He alone was the fullness they needed for provision and sustaining power!

BAKING IN THE BIBLE

Baking has been an essential part of human life since ancient times. The Bible is rich with references to bread, cakes, and offerings made from flour. It symbolizes provision, hospitality, and God's blessings. Although there is indeed a plethora of Biblical stories we could look at on this subject, there is one in 1 Kings that tells us of a widow of Zarephath who met the prophet Elijah during a great drought. Although food was precious and scarce during this foreboding dry spell, Elijah saw firsthand how his needs were met by the power of God, despite how his circumstances appeared.

> *"Then the word of the Lord came to Elijah: 'Leave here, turn eastward and hide in the Kerith Ravine... You will drink from the brook, and I have directed the ravens to supply you with food there.' So he did what the Lord had told him... and stayed there. The ravens brought him bread and meat in the morning and bread and meat in the evening, and he drank from the brook." 1 Kings 17:2-5 NIV*

"Some time later the brook dried up because there had been no rain in the land. Then the word of the Lord came to him: "Go at once to Zarephath in the region of Sidon and stay there. I have directed a widow there to supply you with food." So he went to Zarephath. When he came to the town gate, a widow was there gathering sticks. He called to her and asked, "Would you bring me a little water in a jar so I may have a drink?" As she was going to get it, he called, "And bring me, please, a piece of bread."
1 Kings 17:7-11 NIV

When Elijah added the request for a piece bread, this was her response:

"As surely as the Lord your God lives," she replied, "I don't have any bread—only a handful of flour in a jar and a little olive oil in a jug. I am gathering a few sticks to take home and make a meal for myself and my son, that we may eat it—and die."
1 Kings 17:12 NIV

Elijah then had a response which was a word straight from the Lord:

"Elijah said to her, 'Don't be afraid. Go home and do as you have said. But first make a small loaf of bread for me from what you have and bring it to me, and then make something for yourself and your son. For this is what the Lord, the God of Israel, says: 'The jar of flour will not be used up and the jug of oil will not run dry until the day the Lord sends rain on the land.' She went away and did as

Hey, Wanna Bake With Me?

> *Elijah had told her. So there was food every day for Elijah and for the woman and her family. For the jar of flour was not used up and the jug of oil did not run dry, in keeping with the word of the Lord spoken by Elijah."*
> 1 Kings 17:13-16 NIV

This woman was given hope and a choice to obey. How beautifully she responded to the Word of the Lord! What a supernatural miracle for this woman of Zarephath to find never-ending ingredients for her homemade bread, even in the middle of a drought! The bread sustained them! I can only imagine the renewed joy and wonder she experienced when each morning she found her jars filled to the brim. Although often we despise the droughts in our own life, God is able to show His sustaining power daily to us within them.

OUR PROVISION

It becomes clear time and again throughout His holy Word, barrenness, droughts, and valleys do not prohibit God from His provision. That is often when we can see the miraculous in a deeper way. What care and attention our Heavenly Father gives us. Even in life's bleakest circumstances, we are promised to receive provision and comfort from Him. He indeed is our bread of life! And I just happen to be reminded of it every time I am baking in the kitchen. As I share my baked goods, it is as if I want to share the never-ending joy of God in my life.

So, ladies, do you want to bake with me? Let's turn on your favorite worship music, uplifting podcast or lighthearted story, and try out a new recipe. Let's fill your home with some encouragement and joy! When we are full of joy, it affects all those around us!

MOM'S CHOCOLATE CHUNK COOKIES

1½ cups butter
1¼ cups granulated sugar
1¼ cups packed brown sugar
1 tablespoon vanilla
2 eggs
4 cups all-purpose flour
2 teaspoons baking soda
½ teaspoon salt
1 (24-ounce) bag semisweet chocolate chips — We like using 12 ounce bag chocolate chips + 12 ounce bag chocolate chunks

1. Preheat oven to 350 degrees. In large mixing bowl, beat butter and sugars until light and fluffy. Add vanilla and eggs and continue to beat, until thoroughly mixed.

2. Combine flour, baking soda, and salt. Stir into butter and sugar mixture. Add chocolate chips and with clean hands, mix together; dough may be stiff.

3. On ungreased cookie sheet, drop dough by tablespoon, or use a small ice cream scoop, 2-inches apart; flatten slightly.

4. Bake 10 to 12 minutes or until lightly browned. Centers will be soft, but cookies continue to cook even after removal from oven. Cool

Hey, Wanna Bake With Me?

on cookie sheet, and then remove to large platter. Makes about 6 dozen cookies.

MY BAKING TIPS TO ENHANCE A GOURMET TASTE TO RECIPES:

—*Exchange melted butter for oil.*
—*Use Dutch-processed cocoa powder in place of regular cocoa powder.*
—*Use Madagascar vanilla in place of regular vanilla.*

Happy Baking!

CHAPTER FIVE

superheroes source of strength

Moms are abolsute superheroes.

There, I said it. It isn't Superman, Batman, Spider-Man, and especially not Ant-Man, because he's always creeped me out. In my humble opinion, it is mothers who are deserving of such a title. No matter your birth story, adoption story, or hopes and dreams of becoming a mother, there is nothing like the selflessness, sleeplessness, and sweetness of holding the title, "mother." For now, I know first-hand the wistful woes, vulnerable victories, and unspeakable joys that each day holds. I now marvel less at the Mount Everest climber and marvel more at a mother who is conquering a trip to the grocery store alone with her littles! How I came to this reverent admiration was after an unforgettable solo trip of my own.

Although the lifestyle of full-time evangelism is non-stop to say the least, the extrovert in me thrives in our fast-paced life. So, when I did find myself on a rest day at home in between our flights and revivals, I decided to make the easy one-hour drive to Tulsa by myself with my eight-month-old. It sounded like a splendid idea—a mother-son shopping day—what's not to enjoy? I had it all planned out. A good restaurant, my favorite coffee shop, a quick stop in

Superheroes Source of Strength

Tulsa's best chocolate factory, then we would end the magical day with some shopping. My heart soared with the excitement of what was to come.

On the hour drive, things seemed to be going fairly well. Graham had fallen asleep for most of it, and I listened to an interesting podcast. "This is so easy," I remember thinking with delusion, "Life is too great." Things got slightly more interesting when he began to cry through the Chick-fil-A drive through, but nothing was going to steal my joy at the chocolate shop. I gave him a bottle while we were there and soaked up a few blissful moments of cacao dreams as I picked out a couple truffles for myself.

He fell asleep on our drive to Target, and restored hope surged within me. Podcast back on, prayers of joy were made, and I confidently whipped into the parking lot. When I got him out of his car seat, he woke up. I pushed him along in his stroller for a few minutes, enjoying the aromas of the candle aisle, deciding to splurge on one to fill our home with a fun memory of the day. One thing about my baby Graham, he despises time in his stroller and delights in being held. Soon he began to fuss loudly, but I tried to hold out so I could enjoy a few more aisles of the store. Unfortunately, I wasn't able to enjoy the delightful ambiance because the cries of my child grew more prominent: He wanted out of the stroller and to be held in the arms of his momma. At eight months he already weighed a solid twenty-five pounds, but even still, for sake of my shopping experience, I pulled him out of his stroller and into my arms. As I continued to peruse the aisles of home decor I couldn't afford, stronger than the ache of my arm came the stench of a diaper. For a while, I opted to ignore said smell and bounce him up and down on my hip to keep him content. Yet all too soon I was forced by the power of stench to retreat to the self-checkout to purchase my candle before changing his diaper. I noticed the smell was unusually strong as I retrieved my gift card from my wallet. I must have looked like I was on the struggle train with a baby in one hand trying to get the gift card to work with the other, because suddenly a nice young worker appeared by my side. "Here ma'am, let me do this for you."

"Oh, thank you so much!" How kind he was to help me, I thought. He quickly swiped my gift card, wrapped my candle in the bag and handed it to me. "Thank you," I repeated, feeling encouraged by the kindness still found in the world.

"Yeahhh...." He muttered as he swiftly walked away. On the way to the bathroom to change my son's diaper, I noticed a chocolate looking substance had covered half of my dress. "That's weird," I thought, "I haven't eaten the truffles yet."

My eyes jerked towards Graham's outfit. To my horror, poop had seeped through his whole onesie and quite literally covered every inch of my dress where I was holding him. I almost screamed out loud. We were both covered in poop! Every time I had bounced him on my hip only spread the substance more thoroughly into my dress. No wonder that man tried to help get me on my way as quickly as possible, the smell and appearance was a threat to the store! Horrified, I ran to the bathroom and once his diaper was off, realized all too late—a rookie mistake to say the least—I had forgotten the diaper bag in the car. Using paper towels, I only made the situation worse. Soiled paper pieces now clung onto us, and with pure adrenaline carrying me, I escaped to our car as quickly

Superheroes Source of Strength

as possible. I officially did not have a seat on the struggle train, I owned the struggle train.

I managed to finish changing Graham in the car. I hadn't been a complete failure because I had an extra outfit packed for him, but I had failed to ever hear advice on keeping a back-up outfit in the diaper bag for mom as well! Wipes did their best work, but much was left to be desired. Alas, mother-son day came to a screeching halt as I tried to remain as calm as possible and put my precious baby back in the car seat. Somehow truffles look less appetizing after an experience like that. You must now understand why I admire a mom who is out in public with her clothes fully intact!

Once home, I shared my woes to my sweet husband, and as I hysterically laughed, I threw our clothes in the washing machine. I felt strength fill my heart as I laid our son down for a much-needed nap, lit my new candle, then sat on the couch and opened my Bible. In that moment I was keenly aware there is no magic formula for motherhood. Some days are unavoidably routine and messy, while other days bring an exceeding and unexplainable great joy. Whether we are facing the former or the latter, there is a resource available and strategically brilliant for every career choice and walk of life, including motherhood. It is accessible and it is affordable; it is the Word of God. It is the source of strength anyone and everyone has the equal opportunity to choose, and yet it is a choice we individually must make daily.

Everyone, including superheroes, has a source of strength. The origin of Superman's powers is that his Krytonian physiology absorbs the radiation of a yellow sun and stores it as the source of his powers. Powerful yellow rays of sun bring out his unique abilities while weaker red radiation brings him down to a more human level. Even the superhero who is considered to be the strongest of all is powerless when he is disconnected from his source of strength. I rest assured my strength is not from a strange mutation, and my weakness is not from red radiation, although weaknesses I surely have. However, when connected to the all-powerful source, His strength is perfect, even in my weakness.

THE SOURCE OF THE VIRTUOUS WOMAN'S STRENGTH

It is true, we are only as strong as our connection to the source, therefore I must be daily connected to my Jesus. How often I have read Proverbs 31 and thought to myself, "She's Wonder Woman. There is no way I could measure up to this woman on my best day." It was only recently that a certain verse in the passage popped out at me: *"She girds her loins with strength…" (Proverbs 31:17)*. My first thought was "I'm over here girding myself with a workout skirt so I can walk it off with Leslie," but then my mind quickly sprinted to the Scriptures in Ephesians 6, verses 10 and 14.

> *"Finally, be strong in the Lord and in the strength of his might." (ESV)* and *"Stand therefore, having your loins girt about with truth" (KJV)*.

This virtuous Proverbs 31 woman is simply relying on the strength of her Lord! This is not unattainable, rather this is obedience to His Word. My dear reader, to see her foundation of strength is the same as yours and mine is comfort to say the least. Verse 25 says, *"strength and honor are her clothing."* We are not called to be Marvel's

Superheroes Source of Strength

seductive Wonder Woman, clad with revealing clothing and a flashy sword and shield. We are called to be a woman of God, wearing the whole armor of God and adorned with the fruit of the Spirit.

As far as our little babies and dearest loved ones are concerned, we are the only "superhero" they care about. The greatest gift we can give them is showing by example how to stay connected to the source of our strength. That is how to be a Wonder Woman of worth. It is not found in a perfectly clean home, in the title "Social Media Influencer," nor a closet stacked with the latest and greatest styles, and most certainly not a certain weight or age. Can't you see? It is staying connected to Jesus through daily relationship with Him! He is not an optional source to get us by, He is the Way, the Truth, and the Life. Walking close to Him is the only path that produces a sound mind and a joyful spirit. No, there is no magic formula, but there is a source of strength available daily at His feet!

HIS WAYS ARE HIGHER THAN OUR WAYS

The indisputable and infallible Word of God says in *1 Corinthians 1:25 (NIV), "For the foolishness of God is wiser than human wisdom, and the weakness of God is stronger than human strength."*

This verse is a paradoxical statement illustrating God's ways are not the same as human ways, and God's power is made perfect in what the world perceives as weakness. For example, the apparent "weakness" of Christ's suffering and death is actually the very power of God at work. For it is written, *"Oh death, where is thy sting? Oh Grave, where is thy victory? The sting of death is sin; and the strength of sin is the law. But thanks be to God, which giveth us the victory through our Lord Jesus Christ" (1 Corinthians 15:55-57).* We may feel weak in the wearisome seasons of our life, but we have the Word, we have His Spirit, we have truth, we have Jesus! We cannot forget who we have as our source! Kings bow to our King of Kings. Superpowers, fictitious or otherwise, are at His mercy. Genesis proves His power indisputable. Job reminds us of the vastness of His power. Calvary and the New Birth plan of salvation make His resurrection power personal and available to live inside of us. Jesus is not an optional way to live, Jesus is the only way for us to live! I can join my voice confidently with the Apostle Paul, *"For to me to live is Christ, and to die is gain"* (Philippians 1:21).

There is a comfort and great joy found in knowing who we serve! When we take time to wrap our minds around the honor of possessing a relationship with God Almighty, that knowledge alone gives us a reason to awake each morning with a joy in our spirit declaring, *"The joy of the Lord is my strength,"* (Nehemiah 8:10). We can rest in the confidence that, although chaos might be all around us, His ways are higher than our ways and His thoughts above our thoughts, so we can trust His ways and put on the mind of Christ!

THE GOD OF ALL STRENGTH AND POWER

I find it interesting that tattooing is not a part of mainstream Thai culture and is still reserved primarily for monks, soldiers, and criminals, who believe that skin-art will protect them with invisibility and strength. It is no new thing; from generation to generation, every culture and nation is in search of strength greater than oneself. These folks just believe it will come through a certain tattoo on their body. The pagan people of the Bible times used tattoos to try and appease the gods and get help for loved ones who

Superheroes Source of Strength

had died. Old Buddhist manuscripts claim tattoos are a spiritual anchor so people go to great lengths for that glimmer of hope.

Angelina Jolie, one of Hollywood's elite actresses who is known for her tattoos, has spent time and energy traveling to Cambodia and Thailand to get her tattoos done by a certain Thai monk who uses a more painful process, jabbing into the flesh repeatedly by hand with a bamboo or steel rod. Although, admittedly by Jolie herself, the process is extremely painful, the tattoos promise to hold spiritual blessings, and so, while receiving them, the recipient must pray to Buddha the whole time. How tragic: sending up painful prayers to a pitiful excuse of a "god" who died centuries ago.

Jolie has five lines of Buddhist bindings running down her back and one specifically for her failing marriage in a desperate attempt to bind her marriage together. Mere months after receiving the bindings, her marriage officially ended, reminding us once again, Buddhists bindings and the things of this world cannot keep together a marriage, only Jesus can do that.

Buddhists live their lives in accordance with teachings of a man who has been dead since 486 BC in desperate hope to reach the enlightenment that is promised. It is taught the more suffering, the closer to enlightenment. Yet when a need arises, they must resort to their own power to fix it themselves, for their god is dead. Faith in something does not automatically supply strength; there is only one true source, and all other options will bow before Him on that great day of His returning!

A friend told me recently of a little girl from their bus ministry at church. One day she was watching her mother clean the living room, including the statue of Buddha on the shelf. The chubby man was dusty, so the mother picked him up and cleaned him off. The Sunday school girl looked at her mom and said with sincere childlike faith, "I am so glad I don't have to take care of my God; instead, He takes care of me!" Their god demands suffering in exchange for empty promises. Our God promises to be with us through our suffering.

> *"God is our refuge and strength, a very present help in time of trouble."*
> Psalm 46:1

THE SAME GOD IN NEW ZEALAND

I will never forget a certain church service I was a part of in New Zealand while on a missions trip. As the minister took prayer requests in his enthralling New Zealand accent, he reminded the congregation how others call upon their gods, but we were calling on Jesus, the one who creates all and by Him all things are made. It was no new thing I had heard spoken over the pulpit, so perhaps the impact had something to do with me being halfway across the world, far from my home country. Whatever the reason may have been, it suddenly gave me a deeper perspective when I observed the faith of the congregation. As they began to call on the sweet name of Jesus for their healing and help for their lost loved ones, I rejoiced in knowing He hears and answers the cries of His people. The Spirit of God came in response to the evident faith of the people. Oh, how we can trust Him to carry our weights and worries! I may have been far from my physical home, but never had I felt more at home in the house of God as I felt the same power of the Holy

Superheroes Source of Strength

Ghost sweep over the congregation of believers.

There is no doubt, we all place our faith in something. The atheist believes in the power of self, the Buddhist believes in the hope of enlightenment, the prophets of Baal and Asherah believed calling on their gods could send fire down from heaven, and when the children of God gather, we call upon the name of the Lord Jesus, believing anything can happen! In a little church in New Zealand, I recalled the joy of knowing when we call upon Jesus, it is at that name:

> *"Every knee should bow, of those in heaven, and of those on earth, and of those under the earth, and that every tongue should confess that Jesus Christ is Lord, to the glory of God the Father."*
> *Philippians 2:10-11*

When we speak Jesus, we know,

> *"And there is salvation in no one else, for there is no other name under heaven given among men by which we must be saved."*
> *Acts 4:12*

When we lift our voice, we can rest assured:

> *"In that day you will ask nothing of me. Truly, truly, I say to you, whatever you ask of the Father in my name, he will give it to you. Until now you have asked nothing in my name. Ask, and you will receive, that your joy may be full."*
> *John 16:23-24*

ALL IN ALL

"And whatever you do, in word or deed, do everything in the name of the Lord Jesus, giving thanks to God the Father through him."
Colossians 3:17 ESV

"If you ask me anything in my name, I will do it."
John 14:14 ESV

Dear readers, do we still believe Jesus has saved us, given us new life, restores us, strengthens us, heals us, and gives us the promise of eternity with Him, forever rejoicing on streets of gold? I do! And when we put our mind in remembrance of such a things, we can renew our strength! This is Who gives our strength in our weakness!

CONNECTED, CONTINUING, AND CONQUERING

Marvel's superheroes might be defeated in their weakness, but in our weakness we find the greatest strength of all when we stay connected to the source. I have heard it said, our strength is equal to our problem. If we stay strong in Christ there is no problem that can overtake us!

We conquer, not in brilliant fashion or with choreographed heroics, but by continuing in Christ. We master a sport when we stick to that sport. We master Shakespeare when we stick to Shakespeare. We, dear reader, become strong when we cling to the root of all power day in and day out. Superheroes do not give up when adversaries arise; rather, they lean into their strength all the more. And we, as the people of God, must do the same! No, there is no magic formula, we simply conquer by continuing to cling to the God of all strength.

CHAPTER SIX

idle days in patagonia

The book halted me in my tracks. The color was emerald green with gold lettering, and although the pages were worn, it only added to the charm that was peculiarly its own. Beyond its antiquity and attractive color was the title that caught my attention the most: *Idle days in Patagonia*. I was intrigued for many reasons. The name featured one of my favorite outdoor clothing brands, Patagonia. Entering any store with their brand of overpriced puffer vests and sweatshirts hanging on display makes me instantly feel closer to the adventurous mountains and explorative hikes I so enjoy. I simply love the outdoors! It is my happy place.

Yet Patagonia is more than a clothing line. The definition itself refers to the geographical region that encompasses the southern end of South America, known for the dramatic variety of landscapes. Rivers, volcanoes, glaciers, snow-capped mountains, and forests are all found in the geographic location of Patagonia. You get the picture: a paradisal dream for the true adventure-seeking nature lover. In contrast to the word Patagonia and all it entails was that little word *"idle"* which puzzled me. For idleness, I imagined, could hardly stand in such a glorious location. How could one sit still when such stunning splendor encapsulated each mile?

Upon purchasing the book, I soon dove headfirst into the charm

Idle Days In Patagonia

of the old English and gripping opening chapter. A shipwreck all but took out our heroic main character within the first paragraph, yet somehow in fictitious magic he managed to land safely upon his destination of Patagonia. With intrigue, feeling as if I was almost exploring the land with him, I turned the first few pages with eager excitement. It was incredible: his motivation to keep going in hunger, as if he was almost being fed by the beauty of the surroundings themselves. Before one could get over the awe of flower-filled valleys, the page turned, and new discoveries of ravines and glaciers held their own inspiration. His delight over the constant discoveries brought forth a giddiness in me. And then—all too soon if you ask me—although our lead character still remained in stunning Patagonia, somewhere in the script on the yellowing pages, he became idle in his days there.

I was in shock to read what the next few pages produced. This gifted explorer, who could have chosen any of the waterfall panorama landscapes to establish his home, instead, chose a dwelling place within a field of bristles and overgrown, parched grass. Can you imagine! How could he choose such a dismal location to make his bed when just around the bend was beauty almost heavenly in climate and vision?

I suppose the prevailing philosophy of life, to slip through as easily as possible, strangely enough became his philosophy: to work as little as possible, to acquire as much of this world's goods as possible, to squeeze out as many comforts, luxuries, and pleasures as possible, and to stay alive as long as possible. But what for? Surely not to end up in a field of bristles. He chose the field, but he had only negative thoughts toward it.

The snowcapped, mountainous views required climbing, and choosing to forget his purpose, he had no interest in exerting any more energy. The volcanic oases required distance, and he had weathered enough of his fair share of walking pains. What was in it for him now, anyway? The enchanting forests of greenery demanded effort and suddenly idleness—even if it was in an itchy field—sounded a whole lot better than putting forth any more effort. He chose to manufacture a mindset that required little work: a mindset which allowed his flesh to be at home far from the outlook of contentment and close to words of complaint.

What began as a climactic adventure soon turned to monotony, and I longed to put the book down in utter boredom. What happened to the eager delight to explore new, uncharted waters? Where did his love for exploration and discovery go, anyway?

Upon first arrival, he was joyfully thankful to be present, counting himself blessed for the opportunity to abide in such a place of beauty. Now—in his residency of the prickly, dry grass—he lost the heart of thanksgiving altogether, choosing to give up hope and purpose. Geographically his location had not changed, but mentally it did. There he found enjoyment to dwell upon the negatives, all the while remaining in Patagonia.

OUR PATAGONIA

Before I lecture our character from Patagonia, I must carefully examine my own life. For although we, too, as the people of God have been given beauty all around us, how easy it is to fall into the dry places of mutterings, the tall grass of complaining, and the bristles of complacency. We are indeed living within the blessings, guidance, and salvation of God Almighty, yet too many times I have grumbled words of complaint.

Perhaps your current Patagonia is arriving at the college of your dreams, living in your chosen career, holding a title of your making. Possibly it is the new excitement of motherhood, now having a family to claim as your own. Maybe it is the ministry of your desire, fulfilling the call God placed upon you. Whatever season we may find ourselves in—however glamorous or otherwise—when we are walking closely with the Lord, we are undeniably surrounded by glory.

Yet even living in the fulfillment of our dreams, it is all too easy to set out with joy and acknowledgement of the blessings of God, but as time passes, it is equally easy to wake up and realize we are dwelling in the same tall grass as our man from Patagonia. How could the place we once desired become a destination of dullness? At what moment did we arrive at such a sullen place? Could it really be our negative thought patterns and words that brought us to make our bed here, in a place of discontentment, taking our God-given life for granted?

THE ANSWER

Although our man from Patagonia was undeniably tired, it was more than physical fatigue that brought his life to a place of idleness. What hindered this character from continuing in the very place he once dreamed of dwelling? Could the answer be simple, attainably fixable?

Dear reader, I believe it is! Our man from Patagonia lost sight of thankfulness to the One who brought Him there; he had pushed aside his purpose as to why he began in the first place. Does a thankful mindset and a purpose really have the power to bring us up from our discontented bed of thistles into an energized journey of figurative paradisal scenery? Yes, yes, a thousand times yes—I believe it does!

THANKFULNESS

It was the Apostle Paul, writing under the anointing of the Holy Ghost, who wrote unto the church a simple command:

> *"In everything give thanks; for this is the will of God in Christ Jesus for you."*
> 1 Thessalonians 5:18 NKJV

In *"everything"* can seem a bit of a stretch to our earthly minds. Be thankful—even in heartbreak? Surely, we are excused when we are broken. Be thankful—even in my pain? God must understand we can have a pass when dealing with our wounds. Be thankful—even when I have been betrayed? This must be the exception! Although Paul wrote these words, even he wouldn't get a right of complaint in his shipwreck experience, his dungeon disasters, and being humiliated by those in high position. There are no clauses, no dashes, no parentheses. The command is clear: In everything, in all things, in all ways.

Knowing that every command is written for our good, it only makes sense that the one who created our minds knows what is best for us and what will keep us through all things! It is in those moments we need a thankful heart all the more to keep us from drowning in discouragement. Thankfulness can indeed lift us from our dry place of discontentment!

> *"And whatsoever ye do in word or deed, do all in the name of the Lord Jesus, giving thanks to God."*
> *Colossians 3:17*

SCIENCE KNOWS!

Whether one is on vacation to the Himalayas or stuck inside during a snowstorm, not one of us is exempt from the trap of negative thinking. Our brains are hardwired to focus on the negative, a phenomenon known as "negative bias," making us more attentive to threats and dangers around us. It is scientifically proven that our natural reaction is skeptical and negative, and that we become selfish and inwardly focused.

The first man Adam complained to God after he and Eve disobeyed, the chosen and blessed Israelites complained to Moses in the desert, and Paul found the miraculous church still complaining in the New Testament. No one is excluded!

God in His infinite wisdom and mercy knows the tendencies of His creation; therefore, He gives clear instruction to help our fleshly ways. We are not called to think as others do; we are called to put on the mind of Christ! We are called to be thankful!

> *"Do all things without complaining and disputing, that you may become blameless and harmless, children of God without fault in the midst of a crooked and perverse generation."*
> *Philippians 2:14 NKJV*

WHERE ARE THE NINE?

I can't help but think of the story in Luke's gospel.

> *"Now it happened as He went to Jerusalem that He passed through the midst of Samaria and Galilee. Then as He entered a certain village, there met Him ten men who were lepers, who stood afar off. And they lifted up their voices and said, 'Jesus, Master, have mercy on us!' So when He saw them, He said to them, 'Go, show yourselves to the priests.' And so it was that as they went, they were cleansed. And one of them, when he saw that he was healed, returned, and with a loud voice glorified God, and fell down on his face at His feet, giving Him thanks. And he was a Samaritan. So Jesus answered and said, 'Were there not ten cleansed? But where are the nine? Were there not any found who returned to give glory to God except this foreigner?' And He said to him, 'Arise, go your way. Your faith has made you well.'"*
> Luke 17:11-19 NKJV

Although they equally received miraculous and life-changing physical healing, nine of them appeared to take for granted the holy moment from the healer. Jesus owed these men nothing, yet nine never made an effort to offer a "thank you" to the Master. They were selfish and entitled. Lord forgive me for the times I have acted in the same way. Touched by the Master, yet forgetting how high of a privilege it is to feel His presence in my life. He didn't have to heal me, but how thankful I am that He did!

However, there was one leper who did turn back, unable to let his day go by without giving praise and thanksgiving at the feet of his Healer. Jesus appreciated his sincere appreciation and went one step further: *"Your faith has made you well."* This was a wellness deeper than outward appearance; this was a wellness within his heart. A mind at peace and a contented state of life gifted to him all because of his thankful heart. This inward wellness is the highest quality of wellness, if you ask me!

"A heart at peace gives life to the body."
Proverbs 14:30 NIV

CONFIRMATION OF HIS WORD

Science shows that practicing gratitude activates brain regions associated with happiness, reward, and social bonding, leading to increased levels of "feel-good" neurotransmitters like dopamine and serotonin.

In an article clinically reviewed by Dr. Chris Mosunic, PhD, RD, MBA, we learn these thirteen scientific discoveries: Gratitude and thankfulness encourages positive thinking, improves overall mood, helps manage stress, enhances resilience, improves self-esteem and reduces social comparisons, increases mental clarity and focus, supports heart health, improves sleep quality and falling asleep quicker, boosts the immune system, could reduce physical pain, enhances empathy and reduces aggression, builds deeper relationships through improved communication, and encourages social connectivity.

In another study, they found gratitude may have the power to rewire the brain, possibly by reinforcing positive neural pathways and diminishing the prominence of negative thoughts. This rewiring could possibly occur through a process called neuroplasticity, where the brain changes in response to experiences. Regular practice of gratitude may strengthen the connections in the areas of the brain associated with positive emotions and weaken those tied to negative emotions, possibly leading to a more optimistic and resilient mindset.

This sounds to me like exactly what our loving Father is desiring to give His children. No wonder God has commanded a heart of thankfulness in all things!

NEGATIVE FACTS—WOW!

In the same way positive thinking boosts our spirits up, it is little surprise our negativity, complaining, and grumblings have the opposite effect. Throughout Scripture, God told us to withhold ourselves from grumblings and complaining, knowing the disastrous effects it has on His precious creation.

> *"Be hospitable to one another without grumbling."*
> 1 Peter 4:9 NKJV

> *"Do not grumble against one another, brethren, lest you be condemned. Behold, the Judge is standing at the door!"*
> James 5:9 NKJV

> *"Nor grumble, as some of them did and were destroyed by the Destroyer. Now these things happened to them as an example, but they were written down for our instruction, on whom the end of the ages has come."*
> 1 Corinthians 10:10-11 ESV

Therapists, scientists, life coaches, self-help books, podcast influencers, and counselors are emphasizing now more than ever what the Word knew all along: Negative thinking has led to decreased cognitive functioning. Here is what studies have found: Negativity can also lead to immune system suppression. Since your brain and body are constantly on high alert, all systems get overused and an excessive amount of energy is utilized that otherwise would go toward maintaining your normally strong immune system.

Negative thinking can also cause extreme physical symptoms of anxiety. When you have a thought that conveys a message of impending danger to your brain, your brain signals your body to prepare to escape or fight, and this causes your heart to race, your breath to quicken, and signals other panic symptoms. Recurrent negative thinking can also cause rewiring of associations to fast-track to negative emotions. Anger and hostility in particular can lead to a higher risk of stroke, according to a 2014 study by Everson.

Although it may be second nature to our flesh, surely, we can see it is out of abundant love and kindness toward us God commands us to withhold from complaining. I must admit I have failed on numerous occasions to keep the right mindset; but thank God for His mercy! Today I will choose to have a heart of thanksgiving. Your commands, O God, are always for our good!

PRACTICAL APPLICATION

With all that being true, we still remain human, therefore we cannot escape feelings of sadness or frustration as we walk through life's disappointments. Sometimes we just have a bad day and need the mercy of God to cover us. We also cannot forget there is always a spiritual and practical side to things. We know what the Biblical command and the health benefits are, so how can we implement this into our daily lives in a practical sense?

PRAISE

First, we can break the habit of complaining by praising God even when we don't feel like it. Praise immediately shifts the focus from ourselves—selfishness—to rejoicing in a God who is great above all things—selflessness!

> *"I will praise your name for ever and ever. Every day I will praise you and extol your name for ever and ever. Great is the Lord and most worthy of praise; his greatness no one can fathom."*
> Psalm 145:1-3 NIV

GRATITUDE

We can specifically list the things we are grateful for, putting the remembrance of good things at the forefront of our mind.

> 1. **Gratitude for people**: Paul said in Philippians 1:3, "I thank my God upon every remembrance of you." Being thankful for the people in our lives like family, friends, colleagues, or even strangers who have helped or left a positive impact, brings a thankful mindset to us. We can thank the Lord verbally and write a visual list for our remembrance! What we dwell on immediately dictates our daily outcome.
> 2. **Gratitude for things in our life**: Paul continued in Philippians 1:5, "for your fellowship in the gospel from the first day until now."

Paul mentioned not only was thankful for the people in his life, but the fellowship they bring him. It was not only something he appreciated in the beginning, for he added, "first day until now." He didn't lose his gratitude for the things in his life because time went by! It was a daily gratitude within him. We can show great appreciation even for material possessions, simple comforts, or modern conveniences that God has given us. Hey, I'm sure thankful for electricity, the discovery of chocolate, and sunshine, to name a few! When we begin naming and writing down our blessings, it can be hard to stop!

*3.**Gratitude for experiences**: In Ephesians 1, Paul thanks the church for their faith in Christ and their love for the saints. When we value the opportunity we have to attend church and the high honor to be a part of serving in the ministry, we cannot take it for granted if we live in a heart of appreciation towards it. We can also thank the Lord for simple pleasures that bring us joy—from beautiful weather to major life events and the lessons they've taught us. We can be grateful unto God for trips, vacations, and every open door He has allowed us to walk through. We can show appreciation for the house of the Lord and the encouragement found therein. Above all, as the people of God we have a reason to be abundantly thankful unto Jesus Who has saved us, delivered us, given us gifts, and the promise of heaven. He will withhold no good thing from His people!*

THE GIFT OF THANKFULNESS

I am drawn to those who walk with a pep in their step, those who hold enthusiasm for life itself. I genuinely enjoy being around them! These folks don't have to dine at the fanciest restaurant to enjoy their food. They don't require a touristy beach to enjoy a walk in the sun. Why, it can be a walk through any old neighborhood, yet they're having an evidently jovial time! Each day is accompanied by an excitement to be alive, their world holding beauty no matter their location.

When life gives them lemons, they mix it with sweetness and come up with a new and improved lemonade recipe. Another's negativity cannot bring them down! We all know someone like this in our life. So, what is their secret? What is the common denominator all seem to possess? I have observed one unanimous conclusion: They possess and protect their thankful hearts. They cherish a contentment for their present circumstances, instead of wishing away their reality. And, they have continual communication with Jesus.

Yes, thankfulness pulls us from the tall grass and allows us once again to see the landscape of beauty right within our home, career, family, and church! It is a gift we must cherish and protect lest we become careless: the ability to hold a heart full of thankfulness.

MOST JOYFUL BOOK

It is said by many commentators that Ephesians is the most joyful book of the Bible. How can it be, Paul? To feel joy yet bound within prison! From the pages rise a theme, a mindset that even prison bars cannot incarcerate. Paul kept the mindset of thankfulness that he preached.

I have seen the most humble of homes produce the happiest people. In our materialistic and self-adsorbed culture we might need the reminder: Paradisal places, a certain class of people, and

Idle Days In Patagonia

prestigious possessions on their own cannot bring inward joy. It was Eleanor Roosevelt who said, *"Happiness is not a goal, it's a by-product of a life well-lived."* Paul understood well that our surroundings in themselves are not able to bring happiness and purpose to our lives. He had purpose within a shackled atmosphere because he continued in the ministry and gifting to which God had called him. Even in prison, he reached real people with real problems within a very real church. Throughout the many words of encouragement and correction in his letters, time and again his direction sprung from the parchment: "Church, be thankful!"

I suppose the saying is true in a sense: *"Life is what you make it."* So, dear reader, let us make our life one that is full of thanksgiving. Our homes become a place of renewed beauty, our career becomes newly exciting, and our ministry is restored with purpose. When thanksgiving is ingrained in our mindset, we find there are indeed no idle days in Patagonia!

> *"Not that I speak in respect of want: for I have learned, in whatsoever state I am, therewith to be content."*
> *Philippians 4:11*

> *"Rejoice in the Lord always. I will say it again: Rejoice! Let your gentleness be evident to all. The Lord is near. Do not be anxious about anything, but in every situation, by prayer and petition, with thanksgiving, present your requests to God. And the peace of God, which transcends all understanding, will guard your hearts and your minds in Christ Jesus. Finally, brothers and sisters, whatever is true, whatever is noble, whatever is right, whatever is pure,*

whatever is lovely, whatever is admirable—if anything is excellent or praiseworthy—think about such things. Whatever you have learned or received or heard from me, or seen in me—put it into practice. And the God of peace will be with you."
Philippians 4:4-9 NIV

CHAPTER SEVEN

*if you had a say,
where would this
road lead?*

"*If you had a say, where would this road lead?*" These words plastered in bold font on a billboard in Springfield, Missouri, all but jumped out and popped me in the face. Anywhere? To imagine this highway could lead anywhere of my choosing, where would I pick? An intriguing question to say the least, for I imagine all our responses would contain various answers and bring us down vastly differing roads.

If you would have asked me this question at the beginning of our trek, I would not have hesitated to answer the Grand Canyon, Yosemite, or any other beloved National Park, for that matter. But that was not my response. In this moment, I longed only for the road to lead me home.

Home, where comforts were abundant, rest was available, and pretenses were irrelevant. Although it is our "norm" for our weekly schedule to contain a sprinkling of new hotels accompanied by many miles of commute, somehow within this jaunt the hotel stays seemed less welcoming, the nights shorter, and the hours crept by in the car. I was road-weary and longed for the lights of familiarity.

The church services themselves were worth every bit of sacrifice, I recalled, for I never weary of seeing the glory of God come and minister to His people once again. I feel instantly at

If You Had a Say, Where Would This Road Lead?

home, and I am left in awe within every state, congregation, and nationality as the power of God sweeps into a service to meet with His people. Even still, as much as I loved being an evangelist wife, being apart from home for repeatedly lengthy periods of time had built within me a pull toward home stronger than a pull toward adventure.

Here, my heart longed for our memory foam mattress over the firm bed of a Hampton Inn. I craved our fresh pot of black coffee in my ceramic mug over the specialty lattes in cheap to-go cups accessible on the road. I could almost taste the rich, chocolatey, and healthier snacks my pantry was overflowing with, preferring them over the gas station candy bars. Although I often would bring my favorite snacks and even my fluffy cream-colored blanket from home, somehow it felt a far cry from the real thing when I was holding on to them through airports and car rides.

What is it about home that is a universally inexhaustible subject? Classic Christmas songs harmoniously contain lyrics such as *"I'll be home for Christmas,"* and *"There's no place like home for the holidays."* Congregational church songs emphasize lyrics such as, "I've never been this homesick before!" A house full of one's favorite home-cooked dishes, warm conversations with trusted loved ones, and laughter much like medicine to help ease the years of growing pains are a few of home's charms. All in all, I knew it has little to do with fanciful furnishings and more to do with the feeling found therein.

Yet the question must be pondered, what makes my personal space feel like home? For a certain mattress, tasty snacks, and even splendid dinners isolated to a lonely location hold little value in themselves. My mind raced at the speed of the highway as I posed the question inwardly, "What is that one thing that makes our house feel so homey?"

MORE PRAYER

A few days later—home at last—the answer came swiftly and heavenly in its response. My husband had left early to spend time in prayer at our home church while Graham and I stayed back, his nap time approaching quickly. He had been unusually fussy all morning, which had made me tense, when suddenly I stopped everything, knelt down on his level and said, "Graham, we are going to pray." My fifteen-month-old reached out his squishy hands and I engulfed them in mine.

As I began to pray aloud, the Holy Ghost came into the room like a mighty rushing wind. My sweet son watched reverently as I cried in the presence of the Lord, speaking in tongues, thanking Him for what He was doing in our lives. I lifted my hands in worship only to see through my tears my son's lifted hands as well. There was such a peace that filled the room that Graham—who had been fussy and agitated—quietly began to play contentedly with his toys a few feet from me, stopping to lift his hands every few moments in worship.

When I paused my prayer to wipe my eyes he came bustling over, touched my lips, and did his ASL sign for "more." Although he could already speak numerous words, this was a sign I had taught him from a very tiny age, and he uses it often when he is enjoying something. He didn't want his momma to stop praying—peace was undoubtedly in our midst when momma prayed. I kept on, and each time I would slow down for a minute, he would come

If You Had a Say, Where Would This Road Lead?

and touch my lips, proceeded by his "more" sign. I couldn't recall a more beautiful moment with my son. Our children do not want less of our prayers, our children are longing for more of them. How often had my son done his adorable sign for "more," yet never had it brought me to such tears! Out of the mouths of babes! Our children feel and desire our prayers! The atmosphere shifts when prayer is made in our home!

God impressed upon my heart the answer to my wondering: *"My presence is what makes this a home. Home is where My presence is!"* In that moment I knew home for Graham was already the presence of God, too. Indeed, it is not the specific location of our home on Sixty-Fourth Street, nor is it a specific object that holds power to bring such a calm. It is people and memories that bring value; this was a memory I would cherish with me forever. Home is where the heart is, and Jesus has my heart.

What is a soft mattress or a cozy cashmere blanket without the peace of God reigning within our heart and mind? What is a pantry stocked with chocolatey goodness separated from the salvation of our Lord? At the core, it is close to Jesus where I find the joy and peace as I bustle about cooking, baking, taking care of my husband and son, inviting friends over, taking long walks in the sunshine, and writing in my favorite chair. Without Him, I find no enjoyment in the daily tasks. His presence is home to me!

WHAT DO YOU HAVE IN YOUR HOME?

In 2 Kings, we find a desperate widow who seeks out the prophet Elisha in order to have a very emotional conversation.

> *"The wife of a man from the company of the prophets cried out to Elisha, "Your servant my husband is dead, and you know that he revered the Lord. But now his creditor is coming to take my two boys as his slaves."*
> *2 Kings 4:1 NIV*

This woman's situation was dire and depressing by anyone's standards. She not only felt the consuming sting of losing her husband, but now, bound to the cruel laws of her day, she was bankrupt and unable to pay off her debts. The legal system in Israel would not allow her to simply declare bankruptcy; she instead had to give her sons as indentured servants to her creditor as payment for what she owed. Can you imagine such a plight?

Her fate is almost unfathomable. In between waves of heart-wrenching tragedy, she was now being forced to have her sons taken away like oxen to work as slaves. With grief flowing like waters over the Niagara, she still held a glistening hope: Her husband had been in the company of Elisha the prophet and she believed in the one true God he served. Although it was her only hope, it would prove to be more than enough. After quickly declaring her desperate situation to Elisha, he then asked the woman a somewhat puzzling question: *"What do you have in your house?"*

> *"'Tell me, what do you have in your house?' 'Your servant has nothing there at all,' she said, 'except a small jar of olive oil.'"*
> *2 Kings 4:2 NIV*

If You Had a Say, Where Would This Road Lead?

Her response could have been spoken with embarrassment and frustration. *"I have nothing in my house except one pot of oil."* How easy it is to focus our attention on what is lacking in our home rather than what is left. What is a measly pot of oil when facing such financial bankruptcy? Did he not understand she was having to give her two sons as slaves to the corrupt government? What did household items have to do with anything in a time like this?

Elisha did not focus on the lack of possessions in the house. He did not focus on the looming need of payments, her financial instability, or even the momentary loss of joy itself. His question pointed out not what was plenteous, but rather pivoted to what was present, however meager it seemed. On second glance, the reasoning of Elisha's question is somewhat comforting. He remembered what we often forget: God does not need grand possessions for a miracle; He requires only what we willingly give Him.

Oil is never measly when God is involved. Her oil was described as a jar or a pot—not even a vessel used for cooking—which indicates it was a smaller vessel that held oil for anointing. She may not have had material belongings of any value, but she had one pot of oil. She may not have walked through her home on royal carpets such as were found in the King's court, but she did have the oil. A closet full of the latest Israeli designs were most likely not hanging wrinkle-free in her bedroom, but in the whole scheme of things, it proved no matter; she had the oil, and mixed with obedience, the miracle was on its way!

Then the directive was given by the prophet:

> *"Then he said, 'Go, borrow vessels from everywhere, from all your neighbors—empty vessels; do not gather just a few. And when you have come in, you shall shut the door behind you and your sons; then pour it into all those vessels, and set aside the full ones.'"*
> *2 Kings 4:3-4 NKJV*

Surely at first she could not fathom how this act would save her situation, but even in tragedy and fear, she had strength enough to trust the Word and respond in obedience.

When obedience is mixed with the oil of anointing, the miraculous can happen! As silly as she may have felt, she collected as many empty vessels from neighbors and friends as possible and did just as instructed. She must have been hot, running from neighbor to neighbor, house to house, collecting large vessels. And carrying them? How heavy and cumbersome! Not to mention, what if she was an introvert? She would have been the talk of the town's rumor-mill with such a dire situation, and now to see her speeding around town with empty vessels in hand would have only added fuel to the fire. Yet she did her part in order to see God do His part.

> *"She left him and shut the door behind her and her sons. They brought the jars to her and she kept pouring. When all the jars were full, she said to her son, 'Bring me another one.' But he replied, 'There is not a jar left.' Then the oil stopped flowing. She went and told the man of God, and he said, 'Go, sell the oil and pay your debts. You and your sons can live on what is left.'"*
> *2 Kings 4:5-7 NIV*

If You Had a Say, Where Would This Road Lead?

Once all vessels had been collected, she took her small pot of oil in her home. As her sons brought her one after another, she kept pouring into each empty vessel she had collected. She watched in amazement as the miraculous oil continued to multiply until every single vessel was filled. The oil's outpouring did not cease. It is always God's desire to fill empty vessels with priceless oil!

The prophet then had instructed her to go and sell the oil, and with the profits she would be able to pay all her debt and live on in peace with her sons. Oil held high value in the days of the Biblical text: a precious and necessary commodity for poor and rich alike. Oil was used to keep their lamps aglow, it was needed to make their bread and other foods which sustained them. To the godly, it was for anointing and provision and to the rich, a sign of prosperity. Sure enough, her vessels of oil sold for high value, and because of her obedience, her emptiness was replaced with a cup overflowing, all debts paid off, and her handsome sons continued to dwell peacefully under her roof!

FRESH OIL

In Numbers 11:8, it speaks of the manna having the taste "of fresh oil." It was not something that can be manufactured by man; manna came directly from heaven and needed to be consumed to live. God's provisions are marked with the taste of fresh oil. John 6:33 teaches that Christ is our bread from heaven and that our consumption of Him will sustain and minister life to our souls. We must consume the oil! Psalm 92:10 tells us that King David proclaimed, *"I shall be anointed with fresh oil"* or *"I have been anointed with fresh oil" (NKJV)*. David goes on to tell us that fresh oil is found in the presence of God *(v. 12-15)*. It is there alone that the righteous flourish and find the necessary renewing for our day.

OIL IN OUR HOME

Although every generation holds their own unique style and way of life, nothing has changed when it comes to the essentials for our homes. Although the world may beg to differ, I stand with the Word when I say, our most needful possession is still the oil of the Lord. It is not a preference; we need the oil to live. We must make the necessary sacrifices it takes to cultivate a house of holiness, a place where the Lord dwells. To cultivate an atmosphere where He is welcome, taught, exhorted, and praised must be our top priority!

> *"Hear, O Israel: The Lord our God, the Lord is one! You shall love the Lord your God with all your heart, with all your soul, and with all your strength. And these words which I command you today shall be in your heart. You shall teach them diligently to your children, and shall talk of them when you sit in your house, when you walk by the way, when you lie down, and when you rise up."* Deuteronomy 6:4-7 NKJV

We must desire the anointing oil to have free access, covering our families and loved ones. We must cherish the Word in our home for Paul said in 2 Timothy 3:16-17, *"All scripture is given by inspiration of God, and is profitable for doctrine, for reproof, for correction, for instruction in righteousness: that the man of God may be perfect, throughly furnished unto all good works."*

If You Had a Say, Where Would This Road Lead?

OIL IN MY CHILDHOOD HOME

When I think of my own childhood home, I have never once thought, "If only I could have been raised in a home with a chandelier and fancier leather furniture." How silly to even write such a thought! But often I do find myself sharing with others, "I am thankful for a mom who would wake us up to touch heaven on behalf of a sick loved one. I am thankful for the times my parents got out the anointing oil, a prayer meeting followed, and there was a miraculous testimony on the other side. I am thankful for the times we had family Bible reading together. I am thankful for the times I would hear my mom touching heaven in the other room. I am thankful for her teaching us a love for truth. I am thankful for a home filled with the oil!"

SO, WHAT IS IN OUR HOME?

So, what do we have in our house? Has the budget put a screeching halt to the updates we feel are so desperately needed? I come bearing good news! If we have the oil, we have far more than the riches of this world could provide. Who defines perfection anyway? If we believe in the Word, we know Jesus is the standard for perfection. Therefore, if He fills our home, somehow magazine covers are not the standard any longer. Our home becomes perfect when He is present.

When we can afford it, there is nothing wrong with having lovely and welcoming decorations in our home, but it is not the essential ingredient to happiness and contentment; we find all of that in Him.

If you can hold a prayer meeting in your living room, you have the oil. If visitors feel peace in your home, you have the oil. If your children love the Word and avoid evil, I daresay there is oil in your home! There is no greater gift we can give to our husbands, siblings, friends, children, and family than a dwelling place filled with His presence. Surely such a home is a taste of heaven. So, what is in our home? Let our cry be unanimous, "the oil!"

It must be said of us, our house is a house of prayer. We need the oil of the Holy Ghost saturating our walls and pouring through our daily routines, expressed through conversation. My prayer and desire is as David's was:

"You anoint my head with oil; my cup overflows. Surely your goodness and love will follow me all the days of my life, and I will dwell in the house of the LORD forever."
Psalms 23:5-6 NIV

If you come over unannounced, you will inevitably find much is lacking when it comes to spotless floors, a tidy laundry room, and spotless kitchen. Yet when Jesus is in my midst, the room feels to be lacking nothing; it is one of beauty! Yes, in this busy season as an evangelist wife and mom of a little one, days spent away from our home can seem daunting. But during the weeks in which the road seems a little more rocky before returning again, I will hold this comfort: I am at home with Jesus, and without question, He goes with us every step of the way.

If You Had a Say, Where Would This Road Lead?

IF YOU HAD A SAY, WHERE WOULD THIS ROAD LEAD?

So, to answer the pressing question the billboard offered me, "If I had a say, where would this road lead?" It would lead me straight into His presence. That is my place of safety, comfort, provision, and the very context for my deep-rooted joy.

To put it simply, it leads me home.

"In the house of the righteous is much treasure."
Proverbs 15:6

CHAPTER EIGHT

hidden in the house

It is a question my husband and I have received on numerous occasions: "Why would you want to raise a child in this evil world? Aren't you afraid?" Before I will answer this question, I want to remind us of a story in the Word of God. God's living Word never ceases to amaze me—no matter the time and season, there is relevant guidance, hope, and direction found therein. He keeps us with His Word and in covenant relationship with Him. History may repeat itself, but we can rest assured, God never changes throughout time.

Here in these Scriptures is a perfect example of this truth.

"And when Athaliah the mother of Ahaziah saw that her son was dead, she arose and destroyed all the seed royal.
But Jehosheba, the daughter of king Joram, sister of Ahaziah, took Joash the son of Ahaziah, and stole him from among the king's sons which were slain; and they hid him, even him and his nurse, in the bedchamber from Athaliah, so that he was not slain.
And he was with her hid in the house of the Lord six years. And Athaliah did reign over the land."
2 Kings 11:1-3

Hidden In The House

In the midst of the recorded kings of Israel, we find only one queen who seized the throne for herself. It was unfair by all accounts, infuriating to say the least, for in all reality it was never her place to be. But by evil force, we find her there.

Who was this wicked woman making history? Athalia was her name, the daughter of Jezebel. Being the daughter of Jezebel, surely you learn by example how ungodly one can be. Oh, how much we learn by the behaviors of others inside our own home. Children often mimic things parents and guardians do, and in this scenario we see she chose not to better herself, but to take the wickedness to a deeper level.

This evil daughter of Jezebel heard of her son Ahaziah's death by the furious Jehu and now all that was left of the house of David was only a remnant. Now the question begs to be asked, who were the remnant? Her grandsons were the only remnant left from which the promised Messiah would come.

Those precious grandsons were the only ones left to continue the lineage and make a way for the fulfillment of the prophecy that the Savior would come from the lineage of David. How strangely cruel that Athaliah didn't mourn that her own son had just been killed, she simply used it to further her own ungodly agenda. When she could have loved on those little boys after losing their own father, consoled them through their confused pain, spoke love and compassion over their shattered hearts, she chose rather to rise up and use her time and strength to destroy all the royal seed. The Bible tells us she herself immediately set out to kill every one of her grand-babies. An unfathomable thought to our minds, yet when sin has free course in one's heart, there are no boundary lines to put a stop to such things.

It was all part of her selfish plan to seize the crown for herself, and no one, not even family, could get in the way of her reigning on the throne. Everything about this was contrary to precedent; she was a woman, half-Israelite, half-Phoenician, a foreigner, and not of the seed of David. How the people must have felt shocked and grieved at the injustice of her placing herself on the throne, yet terrified for their lives all at the same time. For with intimidation tactics, including death whenever someone got in the way, she began to rule in the land. She continued to prop up her god, Baal. She wanted nothing to do with God almighty, Jehovah.

In Jerusalem itself altars and images of this empty Phoenician god appeared. Any big or small way to push this false god to children and to lure young people in through glitz and glamour were in place. Their top priority was to make the way of Baal look so common, so beautiful, so dazzling, the "norm" in the culture. What a dramatic and shaking moment for the righteous in Jerusalem! Yet truly there is nothing new under the sun, for it sounds as current as the headlines in the day we are living!

THE CHURCH IN JERUSALEM

In the midst of evil all around, when ungodly agendas seemed to become "what everyone is doing," there was still a church in Jerusalem! And where there is the house of God, there is hope!

God is the one who controls all, it is He himself who sets up kings and takes them down. Proverbs 16:4 says, *"The LORD hath made all things for himself: Yea, even the wicked for the day of evil."* He is not slack concerning His promises! We can rest assured our God always has a plan. God has always reserved himself a remnant. It was the prophet Elijah in utter discouragement and facing death who cried out to the Lord saying, "Lord, I'm the only one left!" But the Lord replied, "I have reserved for myself seven thousand men who have not bowed their knee to Baal (1 Kings 19:18 NKJV)." When it looks as if the enemy is prevailing in our lives, God always has a plan for His remnant! He has provision we know nothing of because our mortal eyes mistake our bleak circumstances for the only way God can work it out. His ways are still higher than our ways! His provision is greater than our provision!

So, if He said that the Messiah—the hope of the world—would come through the lineage of David, then rest assured: even through the remnant, Athaliah's grandchildren, that is exactly what would happen. His promises are forever settled, and he will use willing vessels to accomplish His will.

WILLING VESSELS

In the house of God in Jerusalem, we find the high priest Jehoiada, whose wife Jehosheba had full access to the royal palace. This was due to her relatives: She was a stepdaughter to the evil Athaliah, and she was positioned just where God wanted her to be. What encouragement is found in this passage as it reminds us that it doesn't matter who we are or where we came from, our relatives or our past do not have to dictate who or what we become! We have a choice and do not have to be shackled by the mistakes of others who have gone before us.

Somewhere along the line, Jehosheba got ahold of the truth and joy of God's Word, a love for the house of God, and did not follow in her stepmother's evil footprints. God used her connection and worked all things for good—even her past, because that's what He does when we give our life to serve Him.

While the seed of David was being destroyed, Jehosheba rose up and refused to watch the destruction of the hope of Israel. She snatched the very last baby of the seed royal before he was murdered and hid him, preserving the lineage of David from where our Messiah would come. One woman's choice changed the trajectory of history! One woman made history rising up to kill, another made history rising up to save. I am thankful the people of God are in the saving business!

She hid baby Joash, at first in a storeroom of mattresses within the royal palace but soon realized there is no safety in darkness, so she smuggled that precious baby into the house of the Lord. There he was hidden for six years where he flourished and learned of God's goodness, how to have a servant's heart, and was completely protected from the evil and his enemies of this world.

OUR CHURCH

In this world where evil is still all around, I thank God there is a safe place for us to dwell. A place we are hidden from the evil and darkness that can so easily beset us. If we continue to dwell in the house of the Lord, we will be safe until that wondrous day God calls us home.

Yet to be sure, we can understand the cry of the psalmist when he penned these words in Psalm 73.

"Truly God is good to Israel, even to such as are of a clean heart. But as for me, my feet were almost gone; my steps had well nigh

slipped. For I was envious at the foolish, when I saw the prosperity of the wicked. For there are no bands in their death: but their strength is firm. They are not in trouble as other men; neither are they plagued like other men. Therefore pride compasseth them about as a chain; violence covereth them as a garment. Their eyes stand out with fatness: they have more than heart could wish. They are corrupt, and speak wickedly concerning oppression: they speak loftily. They set their mouth against the heavens, and their tongue walketh through the earth. Therefore his people return hither: and waters of a full cup are wrung out to them. And they say, How doth God know? and is there knowledge in the most High? Behold, these are the ungodly, who prosper in the world; they increase in riches…When I thought to know this, it was too painful for me; Until I went into the sanctuary of God; then understood I their end. Surely thou didst set them in slippery places…How are they brought into desolation, as in a moment! they are utterly consumed with terrors."
Psalm 73:1-12, 16-19

Dear reader, this is why we must be faithful to the house of God. Our perspective changes when we step into the house of the Lord! We have all at one time or another experienced pain, the haunting feeling of rejection, confusion, and even anxieties on every side, but then we walk into His presence. When we take off the spirit of heaviness and, even when we don't feel like it, we put on the garment of praise and speak words of thanksgiving with supplication, something changes. As the singers begin to sing songs of worship to our King, our perspective begins to shift. As the preacher begins to preach from the Word of Life, all else fades away but His presence! What a gift it is to dwell within the house of the Lord!

IT HAPPENED IN THE HOUSE OF THE LORD!

Among the countless miracles I have seen as a full-time evangelist wife, there are two I will quickly share. It was a winter's Sunday night at a church in rural Oklahoma when a sheepish woman walked in shortly after service had started. She held little expression as the songs were sung and even less throughout my husband's message, yet when it came time for the altar call, she swiftly made her way to the front along with the others. The pastor's wife and I began to pray with her, and stopping every few minutes she would tell us, "I'm sorry I can't stop shaking and smiling, I have never felt anything like this before!" We would smile and tell her that she was feeling the beautiful Spirit of the Lord! It wasn't until well after service had ended that she began to share her story. She was on her way to end her life that night, but as she was driving past, something compelled her to stop and come into the church service. Once inside, she found a new hope for living and an excitement that she didn't even know existed, and she added, "Now I don't want to end my life anymore. I have a reason to live." That is the beauty of being hidden in the house! His hopeful presence becomes healing, and the healing finds new life within us! I can't help but think of the song lyrics by Israel Houghton, *"It's not over, it's not ending, it's only the beginning. When God is in it, all things are new."*

A short time after, we were in Tennessee for a weekend where my husband was preaching a revival. At this particular church there was a fourteen-year-old girl in attendance who immediately

Hidden In The House

caught my attention. Though her positivity was evident, even from the outside one could easily see life had been unfair to her. Friday night, she began to share her story with me. Her father had left her and now her stepfather didn't want her either. Where fatherly love should have abounded in their hearts, they had allowed addictions to take over occupancy and left little room for anything else. Her mother tried to love her the best she could, but addictions had begun to take over her mother's heart, as well. Her home life indeed was broken to pieces, but somewhere along the line a faithful saint who was a part of this church's bus route found her and started bringing her to church. The church house, she concluded, was the only place of safety and comfort within her painful world. Any chance to be there, whether it be a Friday night or a Sunday service, was a reprieve for her blistered heart.

All too soon, the last service of the weekend arrived. God's spirit began to sweep across the sanctuary. As worship filled the house, three people approached the pastor to be baptized right then and there! As for that beautiful fourteen-year-old, she found a place in the altar and received the gift of the Holy Ghost. For an hour and a half straight she spoke in tongues, a heavenly language. When she finished praying, the presence of God was shining on her face, her countenance glowing. With tears of joy covering both of our faces, we embraced, and she spoke words that have forever been imbedded into my mind. "I'm not angry at them anymore! I'm not bitter anymore. I just want everyone to experience what I have experienced here in the house of God."

That's why we come to the house of the Lord; we find relationship with our Heavenly Father who cannot hurt us, only heal us. In His house bitterness can dissipate altogether. In His house, the wounds this world has left on us become our testimony of joy for tomorrow! Thank God for access to the house of the Lord!

DAVID'S LOVE FOR THE HOUSE OF THE LORD

It was David who said these oft quoted words,

"I was glad when they said unto me, Let us go into the house of the LORD."
Psalm 122:1

It is little wonder the psalmist penned these words in a heartfelt song! Because of fornication and incest, David was the first in ten generations allowed to enter into the house of the Lord. He did not take it lightly or for granted. Throughout his life he experienced the lowest places and the highest position of man. Even having experienced life in a palace as King with more than one could want of earthly items, this man after God's own heart treasured God's peaceful presence above all. Sure, he was not without his mistakes, but he found the fleeting pleasures of this world ending only in a life of misery. The Lord was merciful unto David's repentant heart, and he would remind us of this truth: Palaces, possessions, and people are no substitution for the house of God! Where our God is, dear reader, is still the only place where we find true fulfillment and peace of mind.

"One thing have I desired of the Lord, that will I seek after; that I may dwell in the house of the Lord all the days of my life, to behold

the beauty of the Lord, and to enquire in his temple."
Psalm 27:4

"Those who are planted in the house of the LORD shall flourish in the courts of our God."
Psalm 92:13 NKJV

"Blessed are they that dwell in the house: they will still be praising thee. For a day in thy courts is better than a thousand. I had rather be a doorkeeper in the house of my God, than to dwell in the tents of wickedness."
Psalms 84:4 & 10

Oh, how it grieves me to see people who have walked with God for years choose to slip out the doors of the house of God, into the tents of wickedness now, when surely He is coming so quickly. Let us gather together all the more as the day approaches!

REVELATION AT THE RYMAN

A few years back my husband and I spent our four-year wedding anniversary in Nashville, TN. After finding a unique coffee shop—because priorities—we went to one of the greatest tourist attractions in all of Nashville: The Ryman Auditorium. As we toured the building, the history began to grieve my heart.

What started with a man simply desiring for a church to be a light in the city of Nashville ended tragically for the soul. This pastor felt the very best and highest quality was needed for such an endeavor—after all it was made to be God's house. Soon the grandeur of the architecture skyrocketed the payments, and the pastor decided that to compensate for building expenses, he would rent it out half the time as a theatre for entertainment. It took only a short amount of time to see what drove the crowds to attend. There were much larger sums of money and people pouring into the building when used for entertainment purposes rather than a church service. How many countless people sacrificed their time for a theatre presentation yet how few showed up consistently for a move of God. How the people never blinked an eye to shell out money for selfish entertainment yet held their pocketbooks tightly to themselves when the offering plate was passed around to give to the Kingdom of God. How quickly the crowds would rise to their feet, lift their hands in the air, and clap with reverent applause when their favorite musicians and entertainers took the stage, all the while staying stoic when the very glory of God filled the sanctuary. Time gave way to the people's desires and even now, one of the most beautiful architectural churches holds within the foyer an alcoholic bar and is used for only entertainment purposes. The crowds still sit on the iconic church pews and in the light of the stained-glass windows. I daresay we all see who they worship.

I went back to our lodging that night with conviction in my spirit and had myself a little prayer meeting. God, help me to never take Your house for granted! The reality is we desire to dwell where we feel comfortable. Therefore, I don't want to make my bed of comfort in the trenches of worldly entertainment. God, help me to be continuously consistent to your house forever!

I walked out with revelation, reminded of the words of Jesus:

Hidden In The House

"Choose ye this day whom ye will serve." I never want it said of my life that my time and money goes quickly and without thought to selfish purposes, yet when it comes to the house of God, I have nothing to give. No worship. No service. No time. No offering. I want to withhold nothing when it comes to service to my King!

WHAT WE FIND IN THE HOUSE:

The prodigal son found forgiveness in the house.
The servants found food enough to spare in the house.
Hezekiah found victory in the house.
Rahab found redemption in the house.
Moses found covering in the house.
David found bread in the house.
Joash found protection in the house.
Anna the prophetess served in the house.
The lame man with four friends found physical healing in the house.
Hannah found her miracle for a child in the house.
Simeon lived till he found the prophecy fulfilled in the house.
The psalmist found peace of mind in the house.
A certain lame man in Acts 3 went leaping and praising with joy in the house.
Peter preached truth in the house.
Prayer was made in the house.
The wise men found Jesus in the house.
Mary and Jospeh found Jesus in the house.

We still find Jesus in the house, so why would we not dwell within His house? Where else would we turn? Life is found therein!

THE PRIVILEGE OF GOD'S CHILDREN

Having a child has changed me in many ways. You could say we have a new passion; we are dedicated to providing for our son the safest home possible. A home as God intended, filled with peace, joy, understanding, unity, righteousness, and love. Simply put, a refuge from the painful things in this world.

Because Graham is our son, he dwells in our house. So when I read in Romans that we, as the remnant, have the privilege of crying, "Abba, Father!"—for we become His children through salvation—it deeply excites me! Because I am His child, I rightfully dwell in His house! It only makes sense that a loving Father would provide for His children a house of refuge in this world. No wonder Jesus told us we must all become like little children to enter into the Kingdom of God. Children dwell in the Father's house! What a gift it is to be His child.

THE ANSWER TO THE QUESTION

So, to answer the lingering question, *"Why would you bring a child into the world at such a dark hour? Aren't you afraid to raise them in such an evil world?"* the answer is really quite simple: We are not raising our child in this evil world; we are raising him in the house of the Lord. We do not have to fear—like Joash, we are the remnant, and we also have a place of safety in which to dwell until He calls us home to receive our inheritance and crown.

OUR HEAVENLY HOME

Not only are we hidden in God's house on earth, John 14:2-3 reminds us of this promise:

Hidden In The House

"In my Father's house are many mansions: if it were not so, I would have told you. I go to prepare a place for you. And if I go and prepare a place for you, I will come again, and receive you unto myself; that where I am, there ye may be also."

This is our comfort, joy, and privilege: If we, as His children, stay hidden in the house of the Lord on this earth, we will dwell in safety until He calls us home. It shall be our heavenly home where we will dwell for all eternity. So, as the darkness indeed does encroach around us, we as His children can put a smile on our face because until that eternal day arrives, we are hidden in this house, blessed by His glory, kept by obedience. Thank God we are hidden in house of the Lord!

CHAPTER NINE

the journey is worth it all

I was fourteen weeks pregnant as I trudged one step closer toward a beautiful bluff in the Smoky Mountains. Despite the twelve hundred feet of elevation gain, I was determined to hike the five miles up this mountain. Perhaps I am too competitive for my own good. Maybe it was pride, since my family was all around me, or it could have been that the challenge itself was simply fun for me, and how I love to have fun. Whatever the case may be, with each upward step, this was my motivation: The view at the top would be worth it all. That really is the greatest motivation. To know the destination, however strenuous or monotonous the journey may be, will be worth it. Without such persuasion, even the strongest would turn back. The "why" is still the strongest form of motivation and achievement.

I had seen just enough postcards and tags on social media to know what awaited us, and I come bearing good news! It did not disappoint our little hiking posse even with our panting breaths, burning legs, and want of gallons of water. A bit weary, we sat on the ledge of the bluff to gaze upon the never-ending mountainous greenery. I kissed my husband, laughed heartily with my sister Aimee, and joked around with my dad and brother-in-law, Andrew. My heart was very full. Once we snapped a few impressive pictures,

The Journey Is Worth It All

it was time to make the journey down the mountain. Arriving safely at the condo, we unanimously concluded the same thing: It indeed had been worth the journey!

WISE MEN'S DETERMINATION

All throughout Scripture are an assortment of men and women who had their own experiences that made seeing Jesus worth it all to them. In the midst of each exhilarating and relatable story arises one that illuminates the pages. They walked with only light from a star and burning faith in their hearts, but that was all they needed. Have you ever thought much about the wise men outside of Christmas? Their strenuous journey is only explored at best in the month of December, their perseverance glanced over without a second thought.

We can look toward the nativity scenes with subconscious thought of, "What an exciting little overnight journey it must have been for them!" Yet the reality is when the Magi finally arrived, Scripture tells us Jesus was dwelling in a home in Bethlehem, separate from our beloved manger scene. Commentaries agree it was at least a year later, if not two, that the wise men from the East made their appearance at His feet.

> *"And when they were come into the house, they saw the young child with Mary his mother, and fell down, and worshipped him:"*
> *Matthew 2:11*

It is more than a Christmas song, *"We three Kings of Orient are bearing gifts we travel afar..."* these were truly kings of the East!

Magi who were educated, brilliant, wealthy, astrologers, and had dedicated their lives to the ancient manuscripts and study of the sky above. These were not pagan astrologers reading some hidden occult wisdom by means of pagan astrology. These were men who were sensitive to the Lord. They sought after God, had poured over the ancient scrolls of Daniel, and studied the starry heavens. They not only knew but believed the prophetic Scriptures that the Savior was coming and would bring an end to bondage and sin.

THE STAR

I can imagine it began as an ordinary night when suddenly they noticed, marked by their consistent and dedicated study, the supernatural and prophetic star!

> *"I shall behold him, but not nigh: there shall come a Star out of Jacob, and a Sceptre shall rise out of Israel…"*
> Numbers 24:17

It was all they needed to spring into childlike action. At the twinkling of the star's light, their hearts soared. "Our King has been born! The Savior of the world is here. We must go to Him. Yes, it might require sacrifice and will consume our time and energy, but this is what our whole lives have been anticipating! We will not go empty handed; we must bring Him gifts of honor. This is the moment we have been living for!" So, they loaded up their camels and brought the most valuable and honorable things fit for a king: Gold, frankincense, myrrh. This they knew would be quite the journey!

Having been reminded of their impressive titles earlier, let us now

The Journey Is Worth It All

capitalize on the relatable reminder that they were also human. They had human feelings, flaws, and of course those faithful personality types. I can imagine with several personalities all traveling together for such a length of time, there could have been many interesting conversations! This journey from the east toward Bethlehem was not for the faint of heart. It probably led them through mountain passes, over sandy desserts, across the Euphrates River, as well as the Jordan River, not to mention many dangers to be faced along the way! Their backs must have been sore from miles of walking and riding the humpy camels. The gold got heavy; they felt the weight of their sacrifices. The weather waffled back and forth. If the desert through which they traveled was anything like the dry deserts of Arizona, their allergies went haywire. Perhaps howling winds stirred up more inconvenient and frustrating moments. I can imagine chilly rains pelted down on them at times. What a long year or two of endurance this must have been! This was a trip one would quickly turn back on if not persuaded of the "why."

And I, with my very real imagination, can picture in a moment with harsh elements pelting against them, those wise men found a place of shelter. Maybe the most extroverted of the Magi piped up first, with frustrations of pain, exhaustion, and heaviness on the forefront of his mind, bluntly saying: "Why are we even doing this? We are all hot. We are exhausted. There has been more sacrifice than I planned for. This has taken much more time than I anticipated. There have been far too many setbacks and more pain than I bargained for. This is hard."

Perhaps when one had expressed his feelings of frustration and discouragement, another one—the more even-keeled of the group—spoke quietly what was still in all of their hearts: "Why are we doing this? For the same reason for which we forsook all and set out on this journey. We came to see Him!"

WE CAME TO SEE HIM

We too have weeks of unannounced pain, serious setbacks, pouring rain, and deep desert sands that slow our steps in our pursuit of His Presence. We surely have had moments when our mind is beaten down with distractions by the time we arrive at Sunday service. For the mother with children, sometimes it is an uphill battle simply getting up and making sure all are clothed and fed before entering the house of the Lord. It would be far less work just to stay home! For the one who goes to church all by themselves with no support from family, it would be easy to turn over and sleep a few more hours, therefore no offense would be made to those family members who do not go on this same journey. For the pastor's wife, the weight of hidden burdens is often more heavy than fellow travelers care to see. For the evangelist wife, another back-to-back week of travel far from the comforts of home can be overwhelming. So why then do we go? The answer has not changed: We came to see Him.

When we step into the sanctuary of God, when we drop our burdens, give freely our sacrifices of praise, bow down before Him and worship our King, we remember the "why." Why we do this, why we live for Him alone, why we walk in our calling. Let us never forget, we have the greatest honor to be in the very presence of the King with all power in heaven and earth. A moment with Him is worth it all!

The Journey Is Worth It All

THE PRESENCE OF A KING

The glaring reality is that it would not have been worth their grueling years of travel if the destination alone was what they were seeking. If their "why" had been scenery, I daresay they would have been greatly disappointed. Bethlehem was far from making the cover of a top tourist brochure. Although little lambs speckled the hills and sun worn shepherds were hard at work, it must have been only the unpleasant odors of sheep farms that most prominently welcomed all weary travelers.

If they would have come seeking big crowds and fanfare alone, once again they would have been disappointed. It was not a crowded church wherein Jesus dwelt. The only folks flocking to the feet of the Holy child was a sleepy mother and a tired father who faithfully tended to the needs of their son. Even the excited shepherds had long gone back to work at the time of the Magi's arrival.

If they would have simply come to enjoy the ambiance and atmosphere of the Savior's earthly dwelling place, how worthless their fatiguing journey would have been! This temporary home must not have had more than a dirt floor and humble furniture. Why would intelligent, learned men spend so much time seeking such a lowly place when their own eastern homes were surely costly and grand? Yet their eyes had no time to critique the style of the building or lack of entertainment, they had not come for such passing things. Their noses were not deterred by unappetizing aromas. Their weary and bloodshot eyes did not even stop to gaze upon the lack of "who's who" that were present. Their knees hardly noticed the cold dirt floor as they knelt before Him. Surely all their minds could process was the joyous reality, "We are in the presence of the King!" Their hearts held no disappointment as they walked into the room and before gifts were given and words were exchanged, fell to their feet in worship before the King of Kings. Did not the Psalmist proclaim such things in Psalm 72:11? *"All kings will bow down before him; all nations will serve him."* They beheld the Savior. In that moment, Jesus was worth the journey. They beheld Him just as He was. He was more than enough!

OUR "WHY"

If location alone is what drives us to church, how discontented we will be. If we fall into the sticky trap of believing, 'if I could just go to so and so's church, I would have a great walk with God and be happy!' There will always be a nicer building, bigger platform, more exciting atmosphere, and a larger city with better coffee and restaurants to offer. But it is not the location for which our souls so earnestly long; rather, it is the Lord of the location!

If our fulfillment is found merely in the crowds at a church, the "who's who" we can tag ourselves next to on the social media posts, the happening music we can move to, this journey of life will come up short. What happens when we cannot be at a location that provides such things? What happens when we walk into a building that has not much more than a dirt floor and two or three people? Will we walk away, saying it is not worth coming here? When we are coming for Jesus, we don't need a certain ambiance to fit our preferences or a certain class of people to worship alongside. People and places cannot give our soul salvation and fulfillment, despite how grand the surroundings prove to be. Let the song of our hearts be: "I just want You—nothing else,

The Journey Is Worth It All

nothing else will do!" When our "why" is simply to worship in the presence of Jesus, we find holy delight whether we are in a small church plant, an overseas crusade, a thriving church in the big city, and everything in between. When our "why" is Jesus, we follow the Light no matter how humble the surroundings may prove to be. When our "why" is Jesus, we keep forging onward even when unpredicted storms sweep our direction. When our "why" is Jesus, we continue to lift holy hands in worship even if our two are the only ones. When our "why" is Jesus, whether crossing the Jordan or crossing a railroad track in a small town, we find joy unspeakable and pleasures forevermore, not because of our location, rather, by result of relationship with our Savior! When our "why" is Jesus, the sacrificial gifts are not carried as a burden but held as an honor to be able to give them to the Highest King. When our "why" is Jesus, our eyes do not have time to nitpick the flaws of our surroundings when we are beholding the Master. Can't you see? In Him we live and move and have our being! We, just as those anointed Magi, are studying to show ourselves approved and walking in the light from above, living for the day we too see Him face to face, bowing at His feet. In heavenly places we will cry aloud with resounding shouts of joy, "the journey was worth it all!"

ALL IN ALL

Dear reader, He is still worth all of our effort for He is the fullness of life itself. Although I was only seventeen years old when I penned these lyrics, now I sing them with an even greater conviction and joy. Of a truth, He is my all in all!

ALL IN ALL

"I learned it in the valley, a long time ago
And I was reminded on the mountain top,
Just the other day
That whatever life may lead me thru
I will sing it in triumph and trial

You are my all in all
You are my all in all
Whenever I think of all you've done
I am reminded again why I sing

Now I've learned that I can trust You
And stand upon your Word
No longer in the darkness, but in the light of truth
So whatever comes against me now
I will boldly declare without fear

You are everything
You are all I need
With all I am I sing
Of who you are"

www.ingramcontent.com/pod-product-compliance
Lightning Source LLC
LaVergne TN
LVHW051246080426
835513LV00016B/1770